Contemporary Theatre Review,
1996, Vol. 5, 3–4 pp. 1–2
Reprints available directly from the publisher
Photocopying permitted by license only

© 1996 OPA (Overseas Publishers Association)
Amsterdam B.V. Published in The Netherlands
b·

CW01507189

Editorial

Franc Chamberlain

Neither *Smoke* nor *Moby Dick* had been performed when Maria Delgado suggested that I look at Wooden's work with a view to publishing a volume of the plays in the *Contemporary Theatre Studies* collection. I read a manuscript of *Smoke* and I found myself engaged with the strength of the vision and the individuality of the voice. I agreed that we should go ahead and publish.

As soon as the decision to publish *Smoke* was reached, Rod Wooden offered me *Moby Dick*, which he was preparing for the Royal Shakespeare Company (RSC), and we decided to link these two plays together in a special issue of *Contemporary Theatre Review* accompanied by a number of supporting articles.

The texts for both *Smoke* and *Moby Dick* were published privately by Wooden under the Crimes Against Theatre imprint in order that a limited number of copies of the text would be available for audience members to purchase. These earlier editions were necessarily of preproduction texts whereas the versions of the two plays presented here include corrections and changes that the playwright made during the practical process of the production period and afterwards.

This is the first issue of *Contemporary Theatre Review* to centre itself around play texts as opposed to critical essays about politics, gender, interculturalism, documentation and performance. This is not to suggest that there is no thinking about these questions in the collection that follows, but that the presentation of the arguments is mostly *through* the play texts of Rod Wooden rather than the critical writing *about* them. The supporting essays are concerned with both practical questions of working on the plays and providing a contextualisation of Wooden's work.

Maria M. Delagdo's article 'Savagery and Fine Words' places the two plays in the context of Wooden's other works and the critical reception to them. Delgado considers the concerns with power and representation that are reflected throughout Wooden's plays through a focus on the disenfranchised in contemporary British society.

Meral Taygun, Artistic Director of the Acting School of Amsterdam, picks up on the image of smoke as an icon of genocidal violence in the twentieth century. The crematoria of Auschwitz may be history but the horrors of ethnic cleansing haven't gone away and have been allowed to erupt once more, less than fifty years after the promise that it would never be allowed to happen again. Taygun's piece is a passionate response to *Smoke* which visions a connection between the sixteenth-century world of the play and the violence of our fin-de-siècle culture. This passionate vision is grounded through a description of the process of staging *Smoke* with students in Amsterdam. Taygun's writing on *Smoke* is complemented by Andrew Wade and Cicely Berry's "Releasing the Play's Voice ..." which reflects on the physicality of the language in *Moby Dick* and the process of working on it at the RSC. Berry and Wade's remarks on the 'anguished doubt' which they find in the world of the play and the 'collapse of metaphysical certainties' which has left '[us] lost in our quest for meaning' connects menacingly with Taygun's cry that we notice the smoke.

Wooden's work is known in the US through the Steppenwolf Theatre production of *Your Home in the West* (1991) and Charlotte J. Headrick's article chronicles the events which led up to that production which she compares with the Manchester production of the play. Headrick is admirably placed to write this story as it was she who recommended the play to Steppenwolf after having seen it at the Royal Exchange, Manchester. Estelle Parsons, who played Jeannie in the Steppenwolf production, completes the issue by writing about the play from the performer's perspective.

Acknowledgements

Rod Wooden has been encouraging, thoughtful, and helpful throughout the process of putting this issue together, meticulous in reading through amended and re-set texts, patient with the time everything has taken, and generous with his time and comments.

Anne McArthur of Maverick Press did the original layout and design of the Crimes Against Theatre editions of *Smoke* and *Moby Dick* and generously gave me copies of her disks to work from so that I didn't have to re-type everything, for which, many thanks.

Pam Dimmock, who re-typed the articles so that I could edit them on-screen, and Oona Campbell, who works wonders amidst a constant avalanche of manuscripts, letters, faxes and phone calls.

ROD WOODEN

SMOKE
AND
MOBY DICK

Contemporary Theatre Review,
1996, Vol. 5, 3–4 p. iii
Reprints available directly from the publisher
Photocopying permitted by license only

Contents

Contemporary Theatre Review,
1996, Vol. 5, 3–4 pp. 3–12
Reprints available directly from the publisher
Photocopying permitted by license only

'Savagery and fine words'[1]
An Introduction to the Plays of Rod Wooden

Maria M. Delgado

This article seeks to produce a general introduction to the plays of the British dramatist, Rod Wooden. An attempt is made to contextualize Wooden's work within the current theatrical climate, and to explain his problematic status as a 'regional' playwright. As well as providing an exploration of the Motifs running through his plays and the theatrical techniques employed by the playwright, there is an examination of the claims made by critics about his work. Theories are posited as to why his plays have generally received more interest abroad than in his native country. The article concludes by examining Wooden's recent publishing venture, 'Crimes Against Theatre'.

KEY WORDS   Rod Wooden, British theatre, playwriting, regional theatre

> I remember John Arden quoting a remark of Tyrone Guthrie's something along the lines of: theatre is a temple and a brothel. It's something I've always believed in.[2] If it leaves out the brothel, if it comes from the head and turns into a theatre of debate, it becomes sterile. Of course there is a place for rationality in the theatre. But if you put that before the rest then the theatre just dries up and dies.[3]
>
> Theatre is about terror and magic. I'm very suspicious about plays which try to tell me something. My plays allow the audience space to make a contribution. Of course that is frightening. They might make a play you don't want them to. But it's more interesting.[4]

The work of Rod Wooden defies simplistic categorisation. At once ambiguously elusive and strongly grounded, prosaic and poetic, it offers the critical establishment no easy or immediate point of contact. When his 1989 play *Your Home in the West* won the Mobil Playwriting Competition at Manchester's Royal Exchange Theatre in 1990, comparisons were made with Sam Shepard, that similarly elliptical chronicler of low-life society. Here was a dramatist seemingly able to work within the moribund formula of realism, whilst simultaneously infusing it with a dynamism and poetry lacking in the more prosaic work of his established London-based contemporaries David Hare and Howard Brenton. Wooden had apparently blasted onto the theatrical scene overnight, and the critics loved it. A former

[1]   The title is taken from the lines of Pegeen to her father in Synge's *The Playboy of the Western World* whilst convincing him of the folly of marrying Shawn, 'a middling kind of a scarecrow, with no savagery or fine words in him at all'. JM Synge, *The Complete Plays* (London: Methuen, 1984), p. 220. It is as a dialectic of savagery and fine words that Wooden would like his own theatre to be seen.
[2]   Rod Wooden, in an unpublished interview with Maria M. Delgado, September 1994.
[3]   Rod Wooden, quoted in Nicholas Pullen, 'Playwright of the West End World', *Guardian*, 11 December 1990.
[4]   Rod Wooden, quoted in Heather Neill, 'Captain Ahab Stages a Comeback', *The Times*, 28 October 1993.

probation officer who had sold his house and car and given up a secure job, living off his savings so that he could dedicate himself to playwriting full time, Wooden offered the press a romantic rags-to-riches story: £10,000 prize money and a one year writing bursary at the Royal Exchange following years of theatrical ignominy and failure.

What critics failed to realize, however, was that Wooden had been a veritable presence on the Northern writing scene throughout the late eighties. Andrew MacKinnon, then Artistic Director of Northern Stage Theatre Company, had commissioned an adaptation of Georg Buchner's *Woyzeck* (1989)[5] which was staged in a double bill with an original one act piece, *High Brave Boy* (1989), on the strength of his first full length play, *Wah Wah Wah Wah, Wah Wah Wah* (1987), which received a rehearsed reading at the Riverside Studios in January 1988. Although *Wah Wah Wah Wah, Wah Wah Wah*, a two act social drama juxtaposing the behaviour of five teenagers in a youth custody centre with the comments of their families and friends, could be read as discerningly political agit-prop urging a fundamental reworking of the youth custody service, its surface idiom belies a sharp observation of the manner in which power structures operate at all levels of society. The emphasis is already on the disenfranchised, those who are silenced or given no voice, those who lie outside the realms of 'official' society. Although the play presents a depersonalised system of 'bosses' and 'inmates' this is no simplistic 'them and us' ideology; rather, as in his most recent work. *Moby Dick* (1993), it gives a blatant exposure of the manner in which the oppressed comply in their own mistreatment. Processes of surveillance and self-regulation are sharply observed, with the teenagers all made painfully aware of their ever-threatened, ever-vulnerable place within the institution's 'pecking order'. The nicknames adopted by the boys offer some protection in a hostile world which would render them insignificant, another meaningless statistic on the outdated computer records. Their nicknames provide them with the chance to re-invent themselves anew, an opportunity to establish a marked presence – as does Micky in *Your Home in the West* – in a precarious world where identities are forever called into question.

Wooden's dramatic idiom has clearly developed. Even *Your Home in the West* which is also noticeably situated within the realist mode, is more sophisticated in its narrative development. Where *Wah Wah Wah Wah, Wah Wah Wah* proves of interest, however, is in the manner in which it points towards the characteristics which inform his more recent work: the emphasis on the orchestration of the stage picture, apparent in the detailed and precise staging directions offered; the creation of a strong sense of place – the decaying Newcastle which also forms the setting for *Your Home in the West* – through a sometimes brutal and uncompromising use of language; a preoccupation with the elusive nature of truth – the inmates all re-write and re-create their lives; and his concerns in 'exploring the dark areas of our existence', in offering for the stage the stories of those 'we push away or don't want to know',[6] all of these are discernible characteristics locatable throughout his work. The structures may have altered over the past five years but these central preoccupations remain.

---

[5]   Dates in brackets are those of initial composition and not those of first production or publication. For production and publication details of all Wooden's work see the chronology at the end of this volume.
[6]   Rod Wooden, in an unpublished interview with Maria M. Delgado, September 1994.

This is visible in *High Brave Boy*, the opening piece of Newcastle-upon-Tyne's Spring 1990 'New Writing North' season and subsequently staged by the 'Off-the-RSC' Fringe Festival in 1992, a tale of two young sisters' induction into the adult world following the death of their mother. Here too language is clearly observed as an oppressive tool, one which is wielded more successfully by the elder Krystal. But even she is 'exposed' as she fails to find the answers to assuage her restless sister Alexis's barrage of questions. As the two girls indulge in role play, enacting the feuds they have witnessed between their parents, a clear and frightening comment is offered on a world where children function as barter, as territory over which their parents' battles are waged, and where their status as products of their parents' flawed value system is clearly discernible. Krystal's attempts to direct the 'performance' meet with a series of obstacles as Alexis tries to deviate from the rules of the game. Until Alexis demonstrates a willingness to compromise – the fundamental determinating factor at the root of all human relationships – the performance cannot progress, its truncated advancement providing a metaphor for the theatrical performance's own uneasy gradation. As with Samuel Beckett's work, the play offers a comment on the mechanisms of performance and the highly complicated relationship between actor and role. As Krystal naively negates her identity as performer in the role of her mother, Alexis finds herself unable to shake-off her own status in the role of her father. She 'dramatises' through improvisation her responses to the events she has witnessed. Unlike the soap opera protagonists whose names they share, theirs is not a glamorised tussle easily reduced to polar opposites. Here the issues are somewhat more blurred, and their realities soiled, tainted, and achingly felt.

One Hundred Feet (1989), originally conceived as a companion piece to *High Brave Boy*, is similarly concerned with the mechanics of theatre. Here a playful exposition of the conventions of the dramatic play is presented for the contemplation of 'the fifth character'[7] – the audience. As the character of David Balfour begins the stage enactment of Robert Louis Stevenson's *Kidnapped*, a series of misadventures occur with actors refusing to accept the unwritten rules which govern the construction of the play text. In the manner of Pirandello's *Six Characters in Search of an Author*, the boundaries between the habitually demarcated stage and backstage areas are decisively ruptured: a woman actor appears demanding a role in a play which, not surprisingly, has no place for her; Stevenson attempts, with increasingly chaotic results, to direct the production along; characters from his other works intrude on the spectacle; actors whose parts no longer fulfil a catalytic or dynamic function demand a change of role. Joined by characters from other works, women self-consciously playing men, and an array of catalysts for action blatantly thrown onto the stage, the characters of *Kidnapped* fumble through the script asking pertinent questions of the conventions governing the construction of character (type), the nature of what is acceptable (ethically, morally, politically and narratively) on a stage and the inherently artificial nature of playwriting. The numerous devices hidden from the audience's view in a 'realist' production are here starkly exposed. When Balfour criticizes Stevenson's 'false dramatic' exposition material, Stevenson tartly responds that 'Dramatic is false for Christ's

---

[7]   Rod Wooden, *One Hundred Feet* (unpublished), p. 10.

sake'.[8] Breaking frame simply destabilises established patterns of dramatic narration, making strange that which we take for granted as the norm or the legitimate. In its recognition of the role of the audience in creating the spectacle, *One Hundred Feet* echoes Barthes' dictum that the text only acquires meaning(s) when it is appropriated by the reader.[9] Stevenson says as much when he states that he doesn't know what the play is all about.[10] He simply creates a shell which is animated by the actor and thus becomes 'something else altogether'.[11]

It is this notion of creating 'something else altogether' which informs so much of Wooden's work. The re-working of established genres (as with classical tragedy in *Medea Media* [1988/9] and *Your Home in the West*) provides a means for interrogating the ideological assumptions upheld by such formal dramatic structures. In *Medea Media* Euripides' tale is transposed to contemporary Newcastle, with Jason recast as a footballing hero who abandons Medea for the more lucrative attractions of his club chairman's daughter. The story is effectively retold by a media employed to rewrite events in a particular, not disinterested, manner. As such the play functions as a denunciation of the media's insidious promotion of 'an excess of trivia',[12] their creation of 'personalities' who reduce the status of the ordinary viewers to second class citizens who cannot share the stars' opulent lifestyle. This is a world where identity is bestowed by an ever vigilant media who determine exactly what matters and what is insignificant and not worthy of exposure or commentary. Reality is thus firmly located within the parameters of representation. Re-write the representation and in effect you re-write the reality.

Your Home in the West also articulates such a view. Micky, the play's male protagonist, constructs a seemingly infallible and untouchable personal, the playboy of the West End world of Newcastle, who perceives himself as a single, unified, unbreakable entity, an image of unadulterated masculinity. Aggression and intimidation are the tools he employs to keep his ex-wife Jean, the rest of his family, and those he comes into contact with, in tow. As the play progresses, Jean interrogates the enigma of Micky Robson and finds it lacking. She locates it in the pre-Oedipal stage of the seven year old Micky. His masculinity is shown to be a social construct, a nurtured performance, which can be traced back to a traumatic episode in the Social Security office where he was abandoned by his mother. His entry into the patriarchal order is crucially located in this event. Since then, as Jean states, 'He has to make people afraid of him',[13] has to believe himself in control. When this is thrown into question, when he cannot bring his mother, Jeannie, back from the dead, then the loss of control commences. His silence marks the emergence of Jean's voice. The feminist critic Hélène Cixous cites an association between silence and hysteria; this is clearly visible in the play's opening acts where Jean is unable to voice her condition, later speaking of having had a fist caught in her throat.[14]

---

[8]   *Ibid.*, p. 18.
[9]   Roland Barthes, 'Death of the Author', *Image, Music, Test*, essays selected and translated by Stephen Heath (London: Fontana, 1977), pp. 142–8.
[10]   See *One Hundred Feet*, p. 22.
[11]   *Ibid.*, p. 23.
[12]   Rod Wooden, *Medea Media* (unpublished), p. 63.
[13]   Rod Wooden, *Your Home in the West* (London: Methuen, 1991), p. 50.
[14]   For discussion of this see Hélène Cixous and Catherine Clement, *The Newly Born Woman*, translated by Betsy Wing (Manchester: Manchester University Press, 1986), pp. 83–97.

Mickey's oppressive regime has, in effect, silenced her. The latter part of the play marks her emergence from this muteness, the removal of the fist. She re-writes the story of Micky's entry into care as told to her by Jeannie. The narration is refocused and shown to be incongruous with the version of events promoted by Micky. Truth is thus shown to be an elusive concept, endlessly re-written according to necessity.

Not that Micky is presented as a 'villain'. The play is clearly situated within a context which presents both him and Jean as slaves: slaves to the bleak social conditions in which they are forced to survive. The West End of Newcastle is perceived as a particularly bleak community – dark, menacing, unsafe – where everybody stays indoors or refuses to leave their home unoccupied because, in Micky's words 'they're shit scared some fucker's going to break in and pinch whatever it is they haven't got'.[15] The insularity generated by such circumstances, where crime offers the only possibility of success and recognition for those who 'can't make a fuckin' pop record' or 'kick a ball about a daft bit of grass',[16] is shown to have catastrophic consequences. The Newcastle setting is, however, not merely a metaphor for the state of England under Thatcher. Nor is the play's Geordie dialect simply a naturalistic device attempting to achieve linguistic 'authenticity'. Rather the regional dialect functions as an assault on the canons of standard English which continue to remain the dominant idiom for (the construction of) 'English' drama. Perhaps the possible radical effect is somewhat mitigated by the classical Aristotelian format of the piece, but the decision to set the play amongst the disenfranchised, among the ghetto class of a particular Northern city and the uncompromising use of the dialect of this class – regional colloquialisms abound, with sentences structured in a manner which draws attention to their linguistic difference – is itself a radical political statement. In addition, this is no Geordie nostalgia play – a genre which has dominated much of the new writing emerging from the region in recent years – but rather a relentless exposure of the violent current running through our present society, a violence which finds expression in the savagery and rage of all of the characters.

In a theatrical climate which only significantly values work produced in and largely by a London establishment, the strongly North East setting and idiom of a number of Wooden's early plays as well as his residency in Newcastle served to pigeon-hole him as a 'regional' figure. Only when recognition beckoned in the form of the Mobil prize was Wooden courted by the system, his plays requested by a stream of directors and literary managers keen to promote the dramatist of the moment. Nevertheless it is worth noting that *Your Home in the West* has yet to receive a London premiere (despite a successful run at Chicago's prestigious Steppenwolf Theatre Company). Additionally, *Diamond* (1990), the play written immediately after *Your Home in the West*, has still to receive a professional production. Its marked deviation from the realist formula of *Your Home in The West* may have something to do with this. *Diamond* presents an elliptical collage of short scenes charting the games of three children, Robert, David, and Lizzie, and their interaction with their respective mothers. The games are played around a select number of props each imbued with a particular resonance which transcends their

---

[15] *Your Home in the West,* p. 42.
[16] *Ibid.,* p. 46.

immediate naturalistic function. The myth of childhood as a time of supposed innocence and unadulterated bliss is shattered through the images presented for the
audience's contemplation. The children's relationships are anything but neutral
and disinterested, but rather imbued with a sharp power dynamic. Each of the
children enjoys a particular status with Lizzie relegated to the bottom of the pile.
Her social indoctrination (the dolls she plays with, the supporting and nurturing
role she is expected to perform to the demanding 'active' boys) is meticulously
demonstrated. Surrounded by images of submission and acquiescence as well as
demands of compliance and subordination, Lizzie attempts to position herself
within a world which seeks, through a complex series of linguistic, economic and
social strategies, to exclude her from power. When such surreptitious measures
don't work, Robert turns instinctively to violence. Lizzie is decisively punished for
not playing the game expected of her, for David ensures the 'accident' is attributed
to her carelessness rather than Robert's frustration. Lizzie is seen to learn the
lesson well, unquestioningly accepting David's version of the injury when bringing the now ostracized Robert a glass of milk. Robert, however, cannot respond to
her warmth – masculine stoicism has already set in. The 1950s childhood world
created by *Diamond* is both delicate and menacing; the rules governing social con-
duct are painfully learned by the children as the logic which has hitherto governed
their behaviour is repeatedly called into question by the society whose values and
codes they are now expected to adhere to.

The pivotal role of formal education in social indoctrination provides one of the
points of departure for *Anti/Gone*, Wooden's 1992 project for the RSC Education
Department. Written for a particular group of Darlington based teenagers after a
series of workshops in the Spring of 1992, *Anti/Gone* offers a harsh indictment on
an education system which serves to promote particular readings of texts. As this
Conservative Government not disinterestedly seeks to convince us of the key
place Shakespeare enjoys within our cultural heritage (as if the 'British' heritage
were a single unified entity), so the narrow-minded schoolteacher employs the
classical text of *Antigone* to similar purposes. Recognising that culture is political,
and that the classroom often offers inept preparation for the world children are
required to function in, *Anti/Gone* provides a series of short, sharp vignettes commenting on cultural appropriation. Here the teenagers are given an opportunity to
state what is habitually discouraged in the classroom. Class is brought into play, as
the expectations of the children are contrasted with those of their middle-class
teacher. Additionally, as in *Medea Media*, the classical tale is appropriated by a media with their own political agenda. As such the text is reduced to a domestic melo-
drama with its easily discernible heroes and villains. In a society where everything
and anything can be marketed and sold, even the girl's defiance (the 'anti' of the
play's title), becomes a valuable and exportable commodity.

The Brechtian non-linear dramaturgy employed in *Diamond* and *Anti/Gone* is a
further feature of *Smoke*: completed in 1993 and staged at Manchester's Royal
Exchange Theatre in the Autumn of that year. The play was inspired by what
Wooden terms 'a footnote in history',[17] Robert Kett's 1549 establishment of the

---

[17]   Rod Wooden, quoted in Alan Hulme, 'Tales from the War Zone', *Manchester Evening News* 18
November 1993.

Great Camp, when 16,000 disgruntled individuals came together in protest against the land enclosures of Edward VI's reign. Although the critics found fault with its fragmented structure and its provision of only 'the sketchiest idea of the historical facts',[18] it was not Wooden's intention to provide a piece of investigative journalism in the manner of a linear state-of-the-nation play. *Smoke* provides a kaleidoscope of fractured interconnecting stories, populated by characters who are not given a concrete past to inform and contextualise the stage developments. The condensed scenes often give the impression of commencing in mid-action, with an array of featured characters often commenting on the action of a previous scene. Apparently incongruous jumps in time provide little expository material for the audience. Such a fissuring of the story-telling process questions the legitimacy of aiming to present a certain linear version of events as 'truth'. The large cast, the unfamiliar names allocated to the characters, the insertion of songs and 'performances' within the play, the excerpting of episodes from a traditional cause and effect structure, all serve to provide the sensation of a multiplicity of voices speaking against one another to provide a plethora of viewpoints. *Smoke*'s protagonists are not the figures which inform 'official' history, but rather those that lie outside it – prostitutes, wanderers, actors, musicians, common soldiers, lepers. Even Kett himself is a distanced hooded figure, seen only fleetingly visiting the troops on the evening before the final battle. The individuals who populate *Smoke* are the dislocated and the marginalised, those whose memory has evaporated as smoke into thin air.

The ensemble work promoted in *Smoke* has largely been lost in contemporary British drama which, for primarily economic reasons, is strongly structured around small casts and the organizing unit of the duologue. Not that the play forfeits the antagonistic merits of the duologue. Characters are pitted against one another – perhaps most significantly the prophetess Wilse and the ambitious Captain, Ysod. Additionally, the conflicts raging within each individual find an analogy in the ideological battles within the camp, and also in the larger conflict between Kett's forces and those of the Earl of Warwick. Not that the play provides a simple binary endorsement of the rebellion as the 'good' oppressed populace rising against the 'evil' oppressors. Rather, *Smoke* offers a stimulating and not altogether easy examination of the contradictions inherent in attempting to define yourself in opposition to an ideology whose language you are necessarily obliged to employ.

The precarious arts funding climate of the 1990s has rendered the production of texts such as *Smoke* an impossibility for anything but the largest subsidised theatre companies. In a situation where economic self-censorship prevails in all work commissioned outside these select companies, the opportunity to provide a play for the Royal Shakespeare Company encourages an exploration of rarely available scenic resources and ensemble work. *Moby Dick*, the adaptation of Herman Melville's 1851 epic novel, undertaken by Wooden for the RSC in 1993, offers a continuation of the techniques employed in *Smoke*. Again the structure is episodic and the cast expansive, with certain characters enjoying a commentary role. The

---

[18] Michael Billington, 'Smoke', 'The Guardian', 22 November 1993.

emphasis is again on ensemble work, with the piece written for a particular group of actors and a particular director, Communicado's Gerry Mulgrew. Fidelity to the novel was abandoned in favour of a process which 're-wrote the novel as a play'[19] appropriate for the nine actors in question. Thus the character of Dundee was created for a Scottish actor in the company; the character of Tahiti (the name of a seaman Melville mentions only once) replaces Fedallah, the Persian prophet of Melville's novel; and the Cook and Pip are amalgamated into a single character. The characters' dialogue was not thus simply appropriated from Melville's dialogue but re-worked and created anew where necessary and appropriate.

Just as the cast offers an amalgamation of different characters, so the scenes depart from Melville's chapters. Episodes in a single scene are complexly negotiated from different sections in the novel. The opening scene offers an excellent indication of this process at work. Here a letter written by Melville to Nathaniel Hawthorne whilst writing *Moby Dick* is incorporated into a sequence which, whilst foregrounding the writing (Melville), also involves the creation of this play, focusing the action on the ship (the Pequod) and indicating the type of men who would willingly risk their lives in what was then the precarious and highly dangerous business of whaling. Phrases from Melville's novel – including the opening line 'Call me Ishmael' – are recontextualised. There is no attempt to 'stage' the opening of Melville's novel because, as Wooden has often stated, 'this is not a staged novel, but rather a play inspired by the book'.[20] Nevertheless, the press reviews displayed an literal-minded obsession with the play's fidelity to the novel, in some cases even listing the 'omissions' they thought most significant, and pompously lamenting its inability to capture the numerous symbolic and/or allegorical levels at which the novel works. Episodes were singled out for consideration without a proper exploration of the manner in which Wooden skilfully re-creates Melville's language, capturing the particular Old Testament and Shakespearean resonances of the novel as well as providing a new commentary on what he saw at its 'clear echoes of classical Greek tragedy'.[21] These 'echoes' are noticeable in the choral work undertaken in the play. There is no attempt to sharply individualise the various crew members, but rather the emphasis is on a community of seafarers, on a group of losers driven frantic by the financial incentive offered by Ahab to exorcise his particular demon: individuality sacrificed in mad pursuit of the whale. Ahab is the pivot of the story, a single-minded obsessive who seeks control over all he comes into contact with. Whipping the crewmen into a state of frenzy, he represents the white whale of the play's title as that dangerous but fascinating 'other' against which they must pit themselves. His destructive obsession sees no limits. Believing himself invisible, he allows no distraction from this fanatical mission. The ships that the Pequod meets are seen through Ahab's eyes as spectres in the mist, only significant for the fresh information they can offer on the whereabouts of the whale. The world of the Pequod is that of conformity to a particular male creed, a particular ideology of rigid values, where domesticity is despised, where the feminine has no place, and where unadulterated misogyny prevails. It is a world which precludes the existence of mystery: anything that

---

[19] Rod Wooden, in an unpublished interview with Maria M. Delgado, September 1994.
[20] *Ibid.*
[21] *Ibid.*

cannot be explained must be destroyed. But in the end it is hubris that is destroyed, and the mystery remains.

Although this most recent play shares characteristics with earlier ones, it would be ludicrous to suggest that Wooden's work has not moved into different directions. Now collaborating from an early stage with directors, and thus finding himself more and more involved in the rehearsal process, the stage directions have become necessarily less detailed. Additionally, re-writes, although still a crucial part of the playwriting process, have become less prominent. *Your Home in the West* enjoyed substantial re-writing before receiving a professional production. *Anti/Gone*, *Smoke* and *Moby Dick* have not been subjected to such an onerous re-writing process. Certainly changes have been made, but they have proved the logical outcome of Wooden's prolonged presence in the rehearsal room, emerging from the realisation that each production is, in effect, a new entity that needs to be negotiated. The versions of *Moby Dick* and *Smoke* published here document the alterations made, offering the possibility of including them in further productions.

Wooden himself recognises the importance of experimentation in his work, arguing that 'the only common feature of all my ten plays is that they are all, to a greater or lesser degree, experiments, an attempt to find out what works and what doesn't'.[22] The fact that theatres 'can never be sure of what they are going to get from me',[23] is one of the reasons Wooden feels he hasn't had as many productions as perhaps he should have done. Critics, he states, 'are at a loss when looking for influences or comparisons'.[24] As such his plays have been compared to the work of a diverse range of canonic authors.[25] Wooden's drama is certainly stylistically eclectic and it is perhaps because the styles never settle into a neat entity that critics have had such a problem categorising and writing about it.

When Methuen, the publishers of *Your Home in the West*, found themselves unable to 'risk' publishing *Moby Dick* or *Smoke* in the current economic climate, Wooden took the decision to publish them himself under the label of 'Crimes Against Theatre' a path now being followed by a number of British playwrights unable to secure a regular contract with the established publishing houses. The title is not insignificant, for it provides a statement on a theatrical climate which Wooden views as itself being a crime against theatre:

All of us, all the time, are committing crimes against theatre. Most acting, most directing, most criticism, most productions, most writing – all of these are crimes against theatre, against the essence of

---

22   *Ibid.*
23   *Ibid.*
24   *Ibid.*
25   *High Brave Boy* was compared to Beckett and Ionesco's work by Peter Mortimer (*Guardian*, 13 February 1990), and to Genet's *The Maids* and Ian McEwan's *The Cement Garden* by Michael Quinn (*The Stage and Television Today*, 15 April 1990). *Your Home in the West* was praised for its 'Strindbergian intensity' by Michael Schmidt (*Daily Telegraph*, 29 March 1990), and compared to Shepard's plays by Rick Levene (*Performing* 26 September 1991) and to the kitchen sink dramatists by Richard Christiansen (*Chicago Tribune*, 7 October 1991) on the play's American premiere. *Anti/Gone* was likened to 'T S Eliot on speed' by Michael Church (*Observer*, 15 November 1992). *Smoke* was compared to Buchner's *Danton's Death* and Brecht's *Days of the Commune* by Hermione Lee on BBC Radio's *Night Waves* (18 November 1993), to Edward Bond's work by Jim Burke (*City Life* 24 November 1993) and to *The Lady's Not for Burning*, *Coronation Street* and *Brookside* by Jeremy Kingston (*The Times*, 23 November 1993). Echoes of Shakespeare's plays and the Bible were located in *Moby Dick* by James Christopher (*Time Out*, 9 November 1993).

theatre, in the sense that they come from the ego, from the desire for financial gain, from the need to satisfy a certain type of audience or a certain social climate. They don't come from the place true theatre comes from. They don't come from making contact with the gods, the gods inside us.[26]

Whether *Smoke* or *Moby Dick* will themselves be viewed as crimes against theatre is, Wooden believes, 'for others to judge'.[27] Both were certainly attempts to create the type of epic and ambitious texts which Wooden views as 'all too rare in contemporary British drama'.[28] A recent commission from the Royal Court Theatre and the interest generated by Wooden's work abroad, suggest that he is not alone in this viewpoint.[29]

---

[26]   Rod Wooden, in an unpublished interview with Maria M. Delgado, September 1994.
[27]   *Ibid.*
[28]   *Ibid.*
[29]   I am grateful to Rod Wooden for his collaboration in the preparation of this article.

SMOKE

a play

by

Rod Wooden

Only in the world I fill up a place, which may be better supplied when I have made it empty.
Shakespeare: *As You Like It*

...appear, shine, and, as it were, die.
Jean Genet: *Letters to Roger Blin*

For
the living
though dead:

Jane
Marina
Agnes Maria

Contemporary Theatre Review,
1996, Vol. 5, 3–4 pp. 15–86
Reprints available directly from the publisher
Photocopying permitted by license only

© 1996 OPA (Overseas Publishers Association)
Amsterdam B.V. Published in The Netherlands
by Harwood Academic Publishers GmbH
Printed in India

CHARACTERS

M	SEVERAL, an actor
M	SYMOND, his boy
F	WILSE, a prophet
M	YSOD, a captain of mischief
F	AGNES, a procuress
F	GRETA, a young woman of the streets
M	JIG, a vagabond boy

M	WYAND, a rogue monk		
M	YALLOP, a discharged soldier	F	STARLING, a beggar
M	MOW, a simpleton	F	KITTLE, a baker
M	THE GAOLER	M	YAXLEY, a man of fire
M	THE HOODED MAN	M	HOWLING, a sentry
F	JACKER, a sentry	M	CLOCK, a thief
F	HUCK, a thief	M	THE PRINCE OF MASTURBATORS
M	THE KING'S MESSENGER	F	THE LEPER

This play has been written for a company of twelve actors, seven male and five female. The first seven listed (ie. SEVERAL to JIG inclusive) should not be doubled. The others may be doubled as follows:

M	WYAND/YAXLEY/CLOCK
M	YALLOP/HOWLING/THE KING'S MESSENGER
F	STARLING/THE LEPER
F	KITTLE/JACKER/HUCK
M	MOW/THE HOODED MAN/THE PRINCE OF MASTURBATORS

The part of THE GAOLER may be taken by either the YALLOP actor or the MOW actor.

CASTING AND COSTUME NOTES

SEVERAL: a travelling actor, 40s. Powerful singing voice, plays the drum. More exotic costume than the others, to denote his profession.
SYMOND: 20s. A dreamer, slowly waking up.
WILSE: 40s. Androgynous – short hair, dresses as a man (Scene Two onwards). Has an 'otherness' about her.
YSOD: 30s, athletic. Wears darker clothes than the others, and gloves.
AGNES: 40s, large. Has lived by her wits.
GRETA: 20s. Carries a bundle (a blanket, folded over) during the early scenes. Has an inner sadness, sometimes expressed as wrath.

JIG: 20s. Full of restless, nervous energy. Often stands with one foot raised, as if in invitation to the dance – hence his name. Plays the pipes (or substitute instrument). Another who lives by his wits.
WYAND: a small, wirey man, 40s. Embittered. Wears a simple habit.
YALLOP: 40s, well built. A professional soldier.
STARLING: 30s. Has a sharp wit, but is inclined to nervousness.
MOW: not obviously young or old. Sometimes speaks with a stutter.
JACKER: 30s. A tough honest, woman.
YAXLEY: 40s. A sharp, eager man.
HOWLING: 40s. Strong, dependable.
THE HOODED MAN: bearded, wrapped in a cloak. Charisma.
CLOCK: crafty.
HUCK: craftier.
THE PRINCE OF MASTURBATORS: long coat reaching to the ground. Pockets full of women's shoes. Craftier still.
THE LEPER: a simple soul but with an inner light.

– swords are worn by **YSOD, YALLOP,** *and* **THE KING'S MESSENGER.** *Everyone else is unarmed, unless stated otherwise.*

– All the characters should be on the thin side – skinny even – except **AGNES, YALLOP, THE KING'S MESSENGER,** *and* **THE HOODED MAN.**

– It is recommended that the play should be performed by a multi-racial company, with at least three of the parts played by black actors.

GENERAL INTRODUCTION

Norfolk 1549. A time of bitterness, great riches, and hunger.

SET AND STAGING

This play was written for a specific theatre in the round, the Royal Exchange in Manchester. If it is staged in a proscenium arch theatre, every effort should be made to break down that separation between actors and audiences which occurs in more conventional theatre spaces – by having some of the action take place in the auditorium, for example. The greater part of the play takes place in a forest, and set design (both inside and outside the playing area) should reflect this.

This apart, set and props should be kept to a minimum, ie. only what is necessary to suggest the scene. If possible, have the set and props for each scene brought on by the actors, or use stagehands in appropriate costume.

COSTUME

The production should eschew all attempt at 'historical accuracy' (whatever that is) – just as the text has done.

No prettified actors, either in costume or facial appearance. Rather a general air of unkemptness: long hair streaked with mud, dirt on the clothing, etc. – these are people who are living out in the open. Costumes should not be restrictive, ie. should allow for a certain physicality of movement.

As a recognition sign, all members of the Great Camp (from Scene Five onwards) should wear green leaves somewhere about their person. Budget permitting, everyone involved with the production – stagehands, ushers, programme sellers – should do likewise.

ACCENT

A Norfolk accent is extremely difficult for non-natives to reproduce and should therefore be avoided unless the actor is from that part of the world. (In any case, a sixteenth-century Norfolk accent would almost certainly be unintelligible to modern ears.) Norwich in the sixteenth-century was highly prosperous, the second city of the kingdom (the equivalent of Manchester or Birmingham today), and the population comprised many people who had come from other parts of England or abroad, some seeking work or riches, others fleeing religious persecution on the continent; the accents of the actors should therefore reflect this.

MUSIC

Musical accompaniment to the songs should be kept simple: use two instruments, a drum (played by SEVERAL) and a set of bagpipes (played by JIG). As the latter are notoriously difficult to play (and the chances of finding an actor able to play them would appear to be almost zero), perhaps another instrument (a flute, or a lute possibly) should be substituted.

THE TEXT

Italicised words or lines indicate emphasis – but not necessarily increased volume. Phrases which *do* need to be shouted, eg. in Scene Twenty, are in CAPITALS.

Pauses in speeches by *the same character* are always indicated by / (a single beat), or by // (a definite pause, two to three beats).

All other pauses (ie. those between speeches by different characters) are shown by the word (*Pause*).

CAMP BUSINESS

This phrase (usually incorporated in the stage directions at the beginning of a scene) is used to indicate various activities – such as meal preparation, washing, chopping wood etc. – which may be improvised by the company in rehearsal or preliminary workshop.

ACKNOWLEDGEMENTS

Some lines at the beginning of Scene Eleven are adapted from 'The Rebels' Complaint', which is quoted in *Robert Kett and the Norfolk Rising* by Joseph Clayton (London, 1913). One of YSOD's speeches in Scene Eleven was suggested by a poem of Pablo Neruda, and a line in Scene Five (repeated in Scene Six) by a similar line in *Lavengro* by George Borrow.

The world premiere of *Smoke* took place at the Royal Exchange Theatre, Manchester, on 18th November 1993, with the following cast:

SEVERAL	Rade Serbedzija
SYMOND	Rhys Ifans
YSOD	Steven Hartley
WILSE	Sorcha Cusack
AGNES	Margaret Robertson
GRETA	Beaux Bryant
JIG	David Fishley
STARLING / THE LEPER	Emma Dewhurst
JACKER / KITTLE / HUCK	Ruth Mitchell
YALLOP / HOWLING /GAOLER /	
THE KING'S MESSENGER	Peter Rutherford
MOW / THE HOODED MAN /	
THE PRINCE OF MASTURBATORS	Jonathan Coyne
WYAND / YAXLEY / CLOCK	Simon Tyrrell

Directed by Braham Murray
Designed by David Short
Music by Chris Monks
Words and Music for songs by Rod Wooden
Movement by Fergus Early
Lighting by Ace McCarron
Sound by Philip Clifford

Company Manager: Helen Thursby
Stage Manager: Catherine Lill
Deputy Stage Manager: Suzi Blakey
Assistant Stage Manager: Sylda O'Brien

The production was made possible by an Arts Council 'Be Bold' Award

SCENE ONE: DAYS OF WOOL

(The sound of wind.
A field, evening.
The burning foundations of a cottage. Beside the doorway, three pairs of shoes, one large pair and two smaller. Kneeling near them a woman, **WILSE**)

WILSE: Even the earth, this huge magnet,
cannot hold us.
We rise as smoke,
as the memory of smoke.

/ (*Touching the shoes*) Boy child, boy child, man. In this safe place. Until.

/ (*Stands up*) Until one day *they* came, and said: is this your land? It is, and everyone's, we said. Where does it end, this land of yours, they said. We looked at them. All men must know their place, they said, as creatures do. What place is that, we said, our place is here. Not so, they said. Where, then? Why, any place *but* here. (*Moving*) Here then, we said. No, further back. (*Moving*) Here then, we said. No, further back. (*Moving*) It must be here, we said. No, further back — try there, (*Gesture*) behind that fence. What fence, we said.

/ Then came the hammering. And still we stayed. Then came the sheep. And still we stayed. Then came the flames.

/ (*Sudden panic*) WHERE IS MY HUSBAND, WHERE IS MY CHILD, WHERE IS MY OTHER CHILD? (*Change of voice*) Safe.

(*Panic again*) SAFETY ON EARTH, WHERE'S THAT?// (*Quietly*) These are the days of wool, they said.

/ The days of wool, I thought. You think they're knitting together, like they're supposed to. But instead of that, they're slowly unravelling.

// I turned my head. And here (*Gesture*) two things of darkness stood, like to: a tall man, and his boy.

(*Off, the faint sound of sheep.*
WILSE *takes the large pair of shoes and one of the smaller pairs, and places them on the ground some distance away*)

(*Speaking to the shoes*) Forgive me this.
/ (*Standing by the small pair, looking up*) This woman, sir. (*A gesture to the front*)
/ (*Goes and stands by the large pair, looks down at the small pair*) Yes, boy?
/ (*Back to the small pair, looks up*) Why do we spare the women?
/ (*Large pair, looks down*) Because of grief.
/ (*Small pair*) Grief, sir?
// (*Large pair*) A woman always wants to prolong sadness. She has to keep sniffing at it, and rubbing against it — like a cat. A man will rush up to it and try to swallow it down all in one go, like a dog. And if he can't do that, he'll run away from it, barking.

// Inside women is where grief lives. It is a useful thing.
/ Inside the darkness in women.
(*She goes slowly back to the smaller pair*)
// Sir?
(*Slowly back to the larger pair*)
// What is it, boy?
(*Slowly back to the smaller pair*)
// You shouldn't attribute human emotions to these people.
(*Goes slowly back to the larger pair, touches the 'boy' on an imaginary shoulder*)
// Come.
(*She gathers up both pairs of shoes and 'watches' as the two figures depart.*
Off, the sound of sheep fades away. Still the sound of wind.
She goes back and puts the shoes down near the doorway)

Husband?
/ Remember when we were children and made shadows on the wall, shapes of animals to frighten ourselves with? The only shape you could do was a huge mouth that ate everything.
/ Remember that, do you?
// I have no husband. I have no child. I have no other child.
// (*Suddenly*) Then let the dogs bark. (*Barks*)
/ Louder. (*Barks louder*)
/ No, louder still. (*Goes to bark again, then stops herself, listens*)
// No, louder still! (*Doesn't bark, listens*)

(*A pause, then she puts the three pairs of shoes on the flames, goes out quickly.*
Lights fade to black.
The flames flicker and go out.
As lights fade down, the sound of wind increases)

SCENE TWO: THE MARKET OF MISCHIEF

(*A market place. Daytime.*
A crowd is gathering: **SEVERAL, SYMOND, JIG, GRETA, AGNES, YSOD, WILSE, WYAND, KITTLE, STARLING, YALLOP, MOW.**
WILSE *is now (and for the remainder of the play) dressed as a man. Noise, music, commotion. Somewhere on stage is a set of stocks (empty). Two characters are apart from the general activity —* **YSOD,** *who sits watching the others, and* **SEVERAL,** *who is preparing his props for the 'play within a play'.*

A number of short sub-scenes are played as part of the general milling about. Note: the stage directions for exits and entrances refer only to the sub-scenes, not to exits/entrances from/into the main playing area.)

   (i)   **(STARLING, WYAND. JIG** *looking on.*)

STARLING : (*To* **WYAND**) Price of a bowl of soup, master?
WYAND : That's begging, what you're doing. Have you got a licence for that? You want to trust in the Lord. (*Goes.*)
STARLING: Ha'nt seen no soup falling from the sky yet.

   (ii)   **(AGNES, GRETA.)**

AGNES: Every soldier back from the war is money. And the lack of it. Every man and woman turned off their land is money. And the lack of it. Every child begging in the streets is money. And the lack of it.
    (**YALLOP** *enters.*)
Money.
GRETA: (*To* **YALLOP**) Looking for business, soldier?
    (**YALLOP** *goes.*)
AGNES: And the lack of it.

   (iii)   (**WILSE** *is listening to* **YSOD.**)

YSOD: I had this dream. The sun was a huge loaf of bread in the sky. It shone like the sun, was warm like the sun. And everything shone with it: houses, streams, even the fields shone. We all basked in the shining. But I was oh so hungry. And when I reached out to touch it, the loaf was too far away. Everything was beautiful and bright, but I was starving to death. All around me children and families were starving, and yet the loaf of bread in the sky kept shining, so beautiful. And as I died, it was the last thing I saw, shining still.
    (*Pause*)
WILSE: I had a dream once. They called me wife in it.
    / But now I'm awake. (*Goes.*)

   (iv)   (**GRETA** *is cradling a wrapped-over blanket.*)

GRETA: (*Going around the audience*) Spare change sir, lady? The child is starving. Spare change sir, lady? (*Goes around repeating this.*)

   (v)   *Simultaneous with (iv)*   **(STARLING, JIG.)**

STARLING/JIG: (*Going around the audience*) Spare change sir, lady? Turned off our land. Spare change sir, lady? (*They go around repeating this, sometimes alternating, sometimes overlapping.*)

   (**Continue both (iv) and (v) through the next scene.**)

(vi)   (AGNES, KITTLE.
KITTLE *is lowering a shutter (a small board which projects out into the street).*
On it, some loaves of bread.)

KITTLE: No one's got any money, I might as well be selling stones.
AGNES: No, it 's cats or rats.
KITTLE: What?
AGNES: What you selling, cats or rats?
KITTLE: What?
AGNES: That's all there is, in't it? I've eaten my way through my house, I've eaten my table, my chair, my cats — now I'm down to the rats.
KITTLE: And after that?
AGNES: Start on the earth I suppose. But that's got a lot of people eating it already, that's why it's disappearing so fast.

(vii)   (WILSE, SYMOND.)

WILSE: ... And a great wind shall come and overturn steeples.
SYMOND: What will be the name of this wind?
WILSE: And it shall throw wives out of bed from husbands, and in her place it shall put a beast of the field. And it shall throw down cities and all manner of governments, and men shall walk naked and see themselves as if for the first time.
SYMOND: This wind. What shall be its name?
   (**WILSE** *inhales and exhales a breath.*)
WILSE: Do you name each of your breaths, brother?
   (**SYMOND** *stares at her.*)
And when all these breaths are joined together ...

(viii)   (STARLING, JIG. YALLOP *watching.*)

STARLING: What have you taken?
JIG: Not a brass fart. We'll be here from arsehole to breakfast-time at this rate. (*Calls*) Greta! Hey, Greta!
AGNES: (*Passing*) Stick to your own trade. (*Goes.*)

   (**GRETA** *enters with the bundle. She and* **JIG** *confer.* **WYAND** *enters.*)

GRETA: (*To* **WYAND**) Spare change, sir? For the child sir.
WYAND: Got nothing.
GRETA: Starving, sir. Turned off our land.
WYAND: Got nothing I tell you.
JIG: (*Coming up behind* **WYAND**) Hey, master.

   (*As* **WYAND** *turns,* **GRETA** *attempts to take his purse.* **WYAND** *turns back, grabs* **GRETA** *by the wrist.*)

WYAND: I'll tan your hinderparts.

(**JIG** *comes up behind* **WYAND** *and takes his purse. As* **WYAND** *whirls round,* **GRETA** *throws the blanket — there is no child in it, it is empty — over his head and pulls him down.* **JIG** *kicks him.* **JIG** *and* **GRETA** *run off into the crowd.*)

WYAND: (*Struggling with the blanket*) Uck you. Uck you, you uggerbays!

    (ix)   (**YALLOP** *is helping* **WYAND** *to his feet.* **KITTLE** *looks on.*)

YALLOP: Well now, master Wyand.
WYAND: Did you see them? Did you see them?
YALLOP: Oh, I seen them master. Like leaves in autumn.
WYAND: Leaves?
YALLOP: In autumn, master. Blowing, in autumn.

    (**WYAND** *looks at him, goes.*)

    (x)   (**KITTLE, YALLOP**)

KITTLE: Varmints.
    (**AGNES** *comes in.*)
AGNES: (*To* **YALLOP**) Looking for business, soldier? (*Points at* **GRETA**) Nice young girl. Come back to the bawdy house.
    (**STARLING** *comes in.*)
STARLING: (*To* **YALLOP**) Price of a bowl of soup, master?
    (**YALLOP** *goes.*)
AGNES: Wasting your breath. Got a deformity, that one — short arms, deep pockets. (*Goes.*)
KITTLE: Varmints.
STARLING: Who is?
    (**KITTLE** *looks at her, goes.*)

    (xi)   (**JIG, MOW. JIG** *is tossing a coin.*)

MOW: What you got there, Jig?
JIG: It's the King's head. Want it?
MOW: (*Excited*) King's head! King's head!
JIG: Hold your hand out. (*Presses the coin against* **MOW**'s *palm.*) There. Now you got the King's head in your hand. (*Goes off with the coin.*)
MOW: (*Staring at his hand*) I got the King's head in my hand. (*Goes around the audience*) I got the King's head in my hand! (*Repeats several times.*)

    (**STARLING** *comes in.*)

STARLING: Let's have a look.
(**MOW** *shows her his hand.*)
Where?
MOW: (*Stares at his hand*) They ... someone ... stolen the King's head! They stolen the King's head! (*Goes around all the others, repeating.*)

(xii)   (**SEVERAL** *gives a drumroll.* **SYMOND** *joins him in the centre and begins sweeping 'the playing area' with a broom.*
The others all gather round to watch the show. **YSOD** *watches both the show and those watching, particularly* **GRETA**.)

SEVERAL: (*Approaching* **SYMOND**) What are you, boy?
SYMOND: Why sir, a scavenger. A sweeper of shit from the the street. (*Finishes sweeping, puts away the broom.*)
SEVERAL: Have you finished, master scavenger?
SYMOND: Yes sir, I have.
SEVERAL: And I say you have not.
SYMOND: How, sir?
SEVERAL: Because you are a sweeper of shit from the street, and yet you have left the biggest *lump of shit* (*Indicates* **SYMOND**) still on it.

(*Laughter /* **SEVERAL** *gives a drumroll.*)

SYMOND: I am no lump of shit, sir.
SEVERAL: No? Then you must be a fool.
SYMOND: Nor a fool either, sir.
SEVERAL: Why then, you must be a thief.
SYMOND: How, sir?
SEVERAL: Because you have stolen a fool's head, and put it on your own shoulders.

(*Laughter/drumroll.*
SEVERAL *and* **SYMOND** *come forward*)

SEVERAL: Now Several the actor, and Symond his boy,
will show you four gentles, their *truths* to enjoy;
and when you have watched them, and grown fully wise,
you'll tell us which of them has told the most *lies.*

(**SEVERAL** *goes off*)

SYMOND: And when you have watched them
we know that you'll join
your hands to your pockets
and take out your *coin.*

(The play begins. **SEVERAL** *plays all four main parts –* **JUDGE, CAPTAIN, BISHOP, LANDLORD** – *wearing a different mask for each one in turn. As the performance progresses, crowd reaction – cheers and boos may be improvised-gradually increases)*

SYMOND: Oh masters look who now draws near: *(Trembling)*
           a man who holds a grudge
           against all those who break the law:
           he'll have their heads — *The Judge.*

(SEVERAL *enters as* **THE JUDGE.)**

JUDGE:	I serve the rich	*(Holds his hand out to the crowd)*
	I serve the poor	*(Holds other hand out to* **SYMOND)**
	I am an honest man	
	and when I come	*(Compares his two hands then*
	to pass the law	*pockets what is in the 'rich'*
	I do the best I can	*one)*

(He puts a rope around **SYMOND's** *neck)*

	The law is like	*(Walks around* **SYMOND,** *wrapping*
	a city wall	*him in the rope)*
	that wraps you right around	
	it shelters you	
	it shelters all	
	until you're tightly *bound.*	

(SYMOND *is completely wrapped in the rope.*
THE JUDGE *bows, goes.)*

SYMOND:	This wall has nearly stopped my breath!	*(Struggling to*
	But now — at last — I'm free.	*take the rope off)*
	But look — yonder *The Captain* comes.	
	What can he want with me?	

(SEVERAL *enters as* **THE CAPTAIN.** *He is slightly padded)*

CAPTAIN:	The army is	*(Beckons* **SYMOND**
	a fortress bold	*then covers him with*
	that keeps you safe from harm	*armour and weapons)*
	just come inside	
	do as you're told	
	we need your strong right arm	

	And if you lose	*(Pretends to chop* **SYMOND's** *arm off, then*
	a limb or two	*then takes away all the weapons and armour)*
	don't spare a thought for that	
	we'll honour you	

and praise your wounds
and then pass round your hat.

(*Removes* **SYMOND's** *helmet and takes a mock collection, then goes off with it*)

SYMOND : God thank you, sir!
You speak the truth!   (*Feeling his body*)
What kind of truth is that?   (*To the crowd*)
Perhaps *The Bishop* can explain
how truth has made *him* fat.

(**SEVERAL** *enters as* **THE BISHOP** *— the padding has noticeably increased.
The sound of a drum is heard (one single note, repeated) circling around the outside
of the theatre.* **WILSE** *and* **YSOD** *acknowledge it to each other, the others appear
not to notice it.*)

BISHOP: I am a lord
but very small
the *Great Lord* lives up there (*Points above*)
inside a house
that's very tall
with miles and miles of air

And if you serve   (*Takes money from* **SYMOND***, puts it*
this smaller lord   *into his 'stomach'*)
the *Great One* you will see
a room up there'll
be your reward
a bigger one for me.

(*He beckons* **SYMOND***, then steps around him and pushes him from behind.
Goes off.*)

SYMOND : But sir, I cannot breathe in here! (*As if enclosed in a small space*)
You couldn't swing a cat!
No use — I'd best come back to earth. (*'Crawling' out*)
But who on *earth* is that?

(**SEVERAL** *enters as* **THE LANDLORD***, wearing yet more padding — he is
enormous*)

LANDLORD: *Landlord's* my name.
Give me some room.
Thank-you. And now some more.   (*Erects an imaginary*
I've sheep to graze   *fence around himself*)
against this fence,
so — no *offence*, I'm sure.

(*Pushes the 'fence' against* **SYMOND** *so that he disappears into the crowd*)

Now where's he gone?
It's quiet here —
as far as I can see
there's fields, and sheep,
and sheep, and fields,
and *me*, and *me*, and *me*.

(*Murmuring increases in the crowd.*
YSOD *suddenly runs forward*)

YSOD: Now see how this man takes you all for a fool — he says he's a lord — he's *The Lord of Misrule!*

(*Pandemonium breaks out as the crowd invades the playing area. They take hold of* **SEVERAL**, *pull out his padding and tear off his mask, which is thrown in the air. Amongst the shouting, two distinct voices can be heard:*)

KITTLE: Commotion! Commotion! Fetch the Constable!
MOW: They stolen the King's head! They stolen the King's head! (*Keeps repeating*)

(*Blackout.*
The shouting dies away, with **MOW**'s *voice being heard up to the end.*
Outside the theatre, the drumming increases in volume)

SCENE THREE: A PIECE OF THE NIGHT

(*A cell. Night.*
Five prisoners: **SEVERAL, SYMOND, WILSE, JIG, YSOD.**
The drum can still be heard, but more faintly. Everyone is now aware of it.)

SEVERAL: When in doubt, arrest the actors. (*Goes to sleep*)

(*Pause*)

JIG: (*To* **SYMOND**) Tell us again. That story.

(*Pause*)

SYMOND: July. Like this month. Evening, just getting dark. I been let out of a dark place, like this place. I'm changed, there's something about me that wasn't there before. Like I'm newly dead.
JIG: (*Quietly*) Before.
SYMOND: There's a breeze. A warm breeze. I'm walking up a street. A row of little houses, all joined together. Starlings coming back to roost on the rooftops. Now it's night.

(*Pause*)

JIG: Then what.
SYMOND: Night. Halfway up the street there's a house I seem to know. Do know. In front of it, dirt.
JIG: Last time you said grass.
SYMOND: No grass, dirt. A child's toy lying in the dirt. Two steps up to the front door. I go up the steps, knock at the door. Then wait.
    // I knock at the door, then wait. *She* comes.
JIG: (*Quietly*) She. (*Louder*) Show us the picture.
SYMOND: *She* comes. She comes like she's been waiting for me all her life.

(*He takes a handful of mud out of his pocket and puts it on the floor in front of him*)

This'll be her. My dark woman of the streets.

(*He makes the mud into the figure of a woman.*
JIG *goes to touch it*)

WILSE: Don't touch her, brother.
    // It's dark. You're walking up a street. Halfway up there's a house you seem to know. Do know. In front of it, dirt. A child's toy, lying in the dirt. Two steps up to the door. You go up the steps to where the door should be. Then nothing.
    // You stand at the top of the steps. It's dark, but your eyes have got used to that. You can see everything clearly. Only there's nothing to see. Where the house was, there's just a space. On each side, the walls of the other houses. But in front of you, a space, like a patch of waste ground. A few bits of straw blowing about in the wind. You keep looking at where your house used to be. But there's nothing. All you see is the night.
    // You step forward. You're part of the night, the darkness. You could be anything, just a shape even. You don't even know where you end and the night begins. You might even be a piece of the night, walking about. When you stop still you could be the earth itself, anything.

(*Pause*)

SYMOND: (*Contained but angry*) How'd you know this.
WILSE: I've been there.
SYMOND: Where.
WILSE: I'm there now. We all are.

(*Pause*)

SYMOND: I'm not. I'm ... I'm where I said I was.
WILSE: Show us then.
    // Show us.
SYMOND: HOW CAN I SHOW YOU WHEN IT'S SHUT INSIDE MY HEAD?
WILSE: Show us.

(**SYMOND** *jumps up, starts beating his head against the wall*)

SYMOND: IT WON"T COME OUT, SEE? IT WON'T COME OUT.

> (**THE GAOLER** *comes in with a flaming torch.*
> **SYMOND** *stops*)

GAOLER: Steady boy. Old wall's harder 'n your head, I do know.

> (*He walks around with the torch, looking at their faces. He does not notice the 'woman' and steps on it*)

> Faces like moons. (*Looking down at* **SEVERAL**) Someone got a bigger drum than you, boy.
> // Bit of quiet'd do me. (*Goes*)

SYMOND: (*Quietly*) Smash it all up.

JIG: What?

SYMOND: I want to smash it all up.

JIG: Smash what.

SYMOND: I don't know. WHAT DOES IT MATTER WHAT IT IS?

> (*Pause*)

JIG: (*Smoothing the mud into a low mound*) Wilse, you show us. What you said.

WILSE: It's here now, look. Just you and the night.
> / And no difference between them.

JIG: Here in this cell?

WILSE: No cell, brother.

> (*Pause*)

SYMOND: I WANT TO FIND THAT PLACE AGAIN I LOST IT.

YSOD: (*Puts his hand over* **SYMOND's** *mouth*) You should have held on to it. You got to make it strong, watertight, so you can walk around in it and feel safe. Yours wasn't strong enough — just a heap of old straw blowing away in the wind.

> (*A pause, then the sound of shouting outside. The drum suddenly gets much louder, then fades. The shouting dies away.*
> **YSOD** *goes over to the cell door, pushes it — it is open. He looks back at the others, then goes.*
> **JIG** *scrambles up and runs after him.*
> **WILSE** *stands, holds* **SYMOND** *by the shoulders, looks at him. Then goes also.*)

SYMOND: Several.

SEVERAL: What.

SYMOND: You awake?

SEVERAL: (*Getting up*) Not so's you'd notice. Come on.

> (*He walks to the door.* **SYMOND** *follows him*)

SEVERAL: (*At the door, looking back into the cell*) Look what your woman's turned into, boy. You been courting a grave.

> (*Lights fade to black.*
> *The drum increases in volume*)

SCENE FOUR: FIRE IN THE STREETS

> (*A street.*
> *Darkness, flickering fires.The drumming fades into the background.*
> **AGNES** *stands apart, in a subdued pool of light. Around her, an ever-changing melee of figures — coming together in groups, separating, coming together again. Amongst them are* **YSOD, JIG, MOW, STARLING, GRETA** (*with bundle*), *and* **YAXLEY**)

(i)   (AGNES)

AGNES: (*To audience*) All that day they were killing sheep. And when night came they roasted three hundred of the creatures in the market place, and shared the meat amongst the populace. And I went wrapped in two great sheepskins, although it was July and hot with the flames.

> (*She strokes the sheepskins.*
> **YSOD** *stands watching her, a sword in his hand*)

And then Ysod came, and gave me a sword — me who had never struck anyone, except with my boot or the back of my hand.
YSOD: (*Giving her the sword*) You're like someone who's laying on her back stroking a rock that's crushing her to death. You can't stroke *pain*. You either kill it or it kills you.

> (*He goes, leaving her with the sword*)

(ii)   (*Another part of the street.***
> **STARLING**, **YAXLEY**. *Both have flaming torches*)

YAXLEY: I've set fire to lots of things. Inns, bridges, rivers ...
STARLING: Rivers, brother Yaxley?
YAXLEY: It's a skill brother Starling, I grant you. Not many have it. And seas ...
STARLING: Seas?
YAXLEY: Difficult. Never had a sea catch yet. A whole ocean, just think of it.
STARLING: (*Ironical*) See the flames from the moon, do you think?
YAXLEY: Are you crazy? How you going to get up there? (*Going back into it*) There's one thing that's harder still. Rain. It goes in the wrong direction.

·(iii) (AGNES)

AGNES : (*Looking at the sword in her hand*) The opposite to no is yes. Isn't it? Not up to now it hasn't been, not in my life. The opposite to no's always been perhaps, or maybe, or not very likely. And I thought: you might get a yes, just once, sometime, and it'll sweep (*Raising the sword*) all the no's away, like leaves down a river. (*Lowers the sword, looks at it*) But then where would you be?

(**STARLING** *comes in with a flame in her hand*)

Why are you setting fire to buildings? If you've got nowhere to live, why are you setting fire to buildings?

(**STARLING** *looks at her, goes*)

(iv) (*Another part of the street.* **JIG, YAXLEY, MOW**)

JIG : What does he look like, Kett?
YAXLEY : No one's ever seen him.
JIG : No one? Then who gives the orders?
YAXLEY : The council. But Kett is the raised finger.
MOW : I seen him. Him a giant, tall as a tree.

(**STARLING** *comes in*)

STARLING : That's not Kett, that's his brother.

(*Laughter*)

Kett's short, round like a barrel. And when he looks at you he squints, (*Demonstrates*) like he's taking aim.

(**YSOD** *comes in*)

YSOD : What in Kett's name are you doing?

(*The group disperses*)

(v) (AGNES)

AGNES : (*To audience*) I used to think that danger was like being locked up in a dark, empty stable — just knowing you couldn't get out, and having to live with the dark and the smell of the horses. But that night I saw that danger is *being let out*, and seeing the horse clearly for the first time, and knowing you'll never ride it. And because of that, you want to kill the rider *and* the horse. And when you've done it, killed them both, and there's nothing left to ride, then it gets *really* dangerous.

(**JIG** *and* **YAXLEY** *go past, carrying a body –* **KITTLE**)

Who's that?
JIG: Baker woman. (*Throws her a loaf of bread. They exit*)

(**GRETA** *comes in*)

GRETA: Agnes! They've fired the bawdy house!

(**AGNES** *looks at her, then turns back to the audience*)

AGNES: The next morning we took our bundles and made our way to the hill above the city, and joined those who were already making the Great Camp. But first, whilst the flames were still burning, we went back to the ruined, filthy houses, and lay down there; not for sleep, but out of habit: the way hunger spills out of your mouth because your mouth can't hold it, and goes roaring round the world, roaring like a wild beast or a huge wind, and then at night creeps back into your mouth, and lays down there exhausted, because it has no other home.

SCENE FIVE : THE MAN ON THE HILL

(*Night. The summit of a hill.*
Below, a city in flames)

SYMOND: (*Coming over the rise*) Several! Several!
/ Lost him.

(*He turns and looks back down the hill.*
Behind him, **A MAN** *emerges from the darkness. He is stocky, bearded, wears a hood. Fastened to his cloak, green leaves.*)

SYMOND: (*Turning*) Sev ...
THE HOODED MAN: It is true — the very air must weigh heavy, the land is so flat.

(*Pause*)

SYMOND: But this ...
THE HOODED MAN: The only hill for miles. (*Looking down*) Such flames...
SYMOND: But those cries — we must help them!
THE HOODED MAN: Help them put those fires out, or start new ones?

(*Pause*)

SYMOND: Help them ... from harm.
THE HOODED MAN: Oh, that. Always recognise it do you, harm?
SYMOND: But ... whose houses are they burning?
THE HOODED MAN: Their own, and other peoples. Know what it is do you, this harm?
SYMOND: Their own?
THE HOODED MAN: When you're empty, it doesn't take much to fill you — a flame can do it. And if you breathe out, and your house burns down ...
  / Now, this harm you keep talking about ...

  (**SYMOND** *stares at him*)

  Here now, is it?

  (*Pause*)

SYMOND: No, but down there ...
THE HOODED MAN: In those flames, is it?
  / Or out there, in the darkness.
  / / And is that darkness not very dark? And is it not truly dark, exceedingly dark, brother?

  (*Pause*)

SYMOND: Who ... who are you.
THE HOODED MAN: Look into the flames.

  (**SYMOND** *looks back down the hill.*
  THE HOODED MAN *goes*)

SYMOND: (*Turning back*) Hey!

  (*A man,* **HOWLING**, *and a woman,* **JACKER**, *come out of the darkness. Both wear green leaves on their coats.* **HOWLING** *carries a sword*)

HOWLING: Hay? It's been a bad year for hay — too much rain, and no hands to gather in the harvest. (*Putting his sword to* **SYMOND's** *throat*) Are you of the Great Camp?
SYMOND: What Great Camp. Has a man passed you?
JACKER: What Great Camp? Here's a creature just fallen from the moon.
SYMOND: Did you see a man now, in the dark.
HOWLING: See in the dark? Only a cat can do that, eh brother Jacker? (*Looking hard at* **SYMOND**) Or a Kett. Do you know that name, brother?

  (*Pause*)

SYMOND: You didn't see anyone?
JACKER: This mooncalf cares more for a shadow than for three feet of steel held against his throat.

HOWLING: Are you of the Great Camp, brother?
SYMOND: Why do you call me that?
JACKER: (*Searching him*) We call all men that now, brother. No weapons.
SYMOND: All men, or just those of your party?
HOWLING: All men?

/ I was turned off my land. Who by, all men? Why. So profits might increase. Whose profits, all men's? What now stands on my land. (*Bleats in* **SYMOND's** *face.*)Who put them there, all men? What keeps them there. Fences. Are they all men's fences?

/ What is worth more than a man's life? (*Bleats in* **SYMOND's** *face*) Do not talk to me of all men. My name is Howling — if it were bleating, would I be worth more?

// Do you know what brought us to this place? Flames in the sky. Who lit them, did all men? Kett says, there is nothing that cannot be changed, *even yourself.**1** Change everything: *first day, then the night.** He does not speak (*Bleats*), he speaks like us, *with the voice of the mud and the dust.** Who will listen, will all men? If we burn down the old life, who will help us build the new — will all men?

(*Pause*)

JACKER: Will you?
SYMOND: (*Doesn't answer*)
HOWLING: Tie his hands.

(**JACKER** *does so.*
HOWLING *motions with his sword*)

Come.

(*They go out.*)

SCENE SIX: TRIAL AT THE OAK

(*Morning. A camp in the woods.*
SEVERAL *lays back singing a song. As he sings,* **JIG** *takes out a set of pipes and begins to accompany him — tentatively at first, but then with confidence.*
GRETA (*with bundle*), **MOW, AGNES,** *and* **STARLING** *are employed in camp business;* **YSOD** *sits apart, watching them*)

SEVERAL: (*Sings*)
    1.   I took myself to the highest tree
            a fair green country under me
            my hand held all that I could see

---

1   **JACKER** joins in on phrases marked *.

but the bird still flew wild
in the wood-oh

2. I took myself to the highest hill
and drank the sky, till I'd had my fill
and when I'd killed all I could kill
the bird still flew wild
in the wood-oh

(*Chorus*)

The owl in the wood, the lark on the hill
the bird flies wild as my heart stands still
and tall as you build your tower of blood
you'll never be free of the bird
in the wood

3. I took myself to the highest star
and looked on the world so bright and far
and all I could see in the place where you stood
was a bird flying wild in a deep, dark wood

(*Repeat chorus*)

(*The song ends.* **JIG** *plays a few more bars, then stops*)

SEVERAL: Steal them pipes, boy?
JIG: (*Doesn't answer*)
STARLING: (*To* **MOW**) What you chewing?
MOW: Brother sheep.
STARLING: (*To no-one in particular*) This ground's too good to have sheep jamming up and down on it.
JIG: Or birds shitting on it, brother Starling.
GRETA: (*Setting down a bucket*) Is there no end to carrying water?
AGNES: Better that than earth.
SEVERAL: Steal them pipes, boy?
JIG: Got 'em off brother sheep.

(**JACKER** *and* **HOWLING** *bring in* **SYMOND**, *who is barefoot.* **JACKER** *carries his boots, which she puts down nearby.* **HOWLING** *still has the sword.* **WYAND** *enters behind them, stands watching*)

JACKER: Spy.

(*The others gather round, except* **SEVERAL** *and* **YSOD**)

STARLING: Seen that boy before.
HOWLING: (*Prodding* **SYMOND** *with the sword*) Speak, spy.
MOW: Speak, spy.

SYMOND: (*Catching sight of* **SEVERAL**) Hey, Sev ...
SEVERAL: Speak, spy.

(*Pause/murmuring*)

AGNES: Where are you from, brother.
SYMOND: I come ... from a far country.
DIFFERENT VOICES: Where? Where?
SYMOND: I come from a village ...
AGNES: No, speak to us from out of your *life*.

(*Pause/murmuring*)

SYMOND: I come out of mud and dust.

(*Silence*)

I am one who builds a house for the whole man ...
STARLING: Are you a carpenter?
SYMOND: No, a shoemaker. For is the whole man's being not lodged in his shoes?

(*Laughter*)

My master died. I had no roof. And then I heard of a great city, with upwards of sixteen thousand people. And I thought, that's thirty two thousand feet.

(*Laughter*)

STARLING: And ten thousand of them belong to shoemakers.

(*Laughter*)

SYMOND: Just so.
/ So I found a new trade (*Looking at* **SEVERAL**) ... and a new master. But I was caught in riot and thrown in gaol. *Unjustly*. And when the fire came I made good my escape, and climbed this hill. And when I looked back and saw the flames rising in the night air I felt very cold, truly cold, exceedingly cold, brothers.

(*A tremor runs through the crowd.*
SYMOND *looks bewildered*)

DIFFERENT VOICES: A prophet! A prophet!
WYAND: But he is a *false* prophet. For have we come to this Great Camp to still follow the old falsehoods of field and wood? Are we not here to build a new city, a city of the heart? There is only one prophet in this Camp, and that is ...
DIFFERENT VOICES: Kett! Kett!
WYAND: *It is not Kett it is the Lord.*

(*Silence*)

You, with your talk of prophets. This man is a false prophet, he should be hanged.
YSOD: And is Kett then a false prophet? And should he not be hanged also?

(*Murmuring in the crowd*)

AGNES: (*Scornfully*) This boy is no prophet, he is a shoemaker.

(*Laughter*)

HOWLING: (*To the crowd*) What say you, is he a prophet?
STARLING: (*Examining* **SYMOND's** *boots*) He must be, for his boots are holy.

(*Laughter*)

VOICES: Free him, free him.

(**HOWLING** *lowers his sword, motions* **SYMOND** *to put on his boots.*
As the crowd drifts away, **YSOD** *goes up to* **GRETA,** *takes her chin in his hand,*
looks at her; then goes.
SYMOND, SEVERAL, *and* **GRETA** *are left.*
JIG *sits apart, juggling with some coloured balls*)

SYMOND: Several?
SEVERAL: (*Getting up*) Don't need two boys. This one (*Indicates* **JIG**) plays the
pipes. (*Goes*)
GRETA: (*Handing* **SYMOND** *a cup*) Drink, brother.
SYMOND: (*Doing so*) What is it, this Great Camp?
GRETA: You a traveller, and not heard of the Great Camp?

(*Pause*)

SYMOND: Why did they call me a prophet?
GRETA: Because you used certain words, brother, that are only used by prophets.
SYMOND: This is a strange country.
GRETA: Is it strange, brother, to be looking for prophets? Is that not what all
men do?
SYMOND: Is there such thing as a prophet?
GRETA: Some say Kett is a prophet. Others say he is greater than that, for a
prophet only paves the way. Some say Wilse is a prophet. And some say that the
Great Camp should cast down all prophets , and men should live only by what is
in their hearts, and not by the tongues of prophets.
SYMOND: And women too?
     // That man who touched you, was he … ?
GRETA: Ysod? No prophet, brother.

(*Pause*)

SYMOND: Why did you come to this place?
GRETA: I was brought here, brother, to comfort the men.

(*Pause*)

SYMOND: Do they give you coin?
GRETA: They give me food and drink, brother.
SYMOND: But that is no more than we give to the beasts of the field, and they have no roof over their heads.
GRETA: And no more do we in the Great Camp, brother. But we have bread, and eggs, and ale, where before we had only beans, and oats, and acorns. And we have brother sheep for meat, and brother cow for milk...
SYMOND: Should that not be sister cow?
GRETA: No, for in brother and sister there is a difference of the flesh, but between brother and brother there is none. So brother cow, brother.
SYMOND: But between man and woman, is there not a difference of the flesh?
GRETA: You play with words, brother. And these are fine things which you juggle and throw in the air, like a trickster at a carnival. Speak from your heart, brother. (*She goes.*)
SYMOND: (*To* **JIG**) What does she say?
JIG: (*Throwing balls into the air and catching them*) She says ... that you are neither he, she, it, nor yet the old woman, brother.

(*Pause*)

SYMOND: What is the name of this place?
JIG: It goes by the name of Thorpe Wood.
SYMOND: (*Musing*) Thorpe Wood, by the city of ...
JIG: (*Interrupting*) By the city of no name, brother. (*Getting up*) For are we of the Great Camp to live by old names? Is not the world to be turned on its head, and a new language born? Perhaps that city will die, and a new city arise here in these woods. And what are names, but hooks on which to hang a man? No more names of cities, brother.
SYMOND: And men, shall they no longer have names?
JIG: Only for convenience, brother. Such as you might say to me, set down that pail, Jig — which would avoid having a multitude of brothers in the vicinity all setting down pails at the same time. But only for that. Not for rank, stank, stink or station, brother.

(**WYAND** *comes in*)

WYAND: My purse, you uggerbay.
JIG: My? My's dead. A greedy, ugly, puking thing — it died o' Saturday. See — here's a farthing for the funeral.

(*He flings a coin at* **WYAND**. *As* **WYAND** *stoops to pick it up,* **JIG** *catches him by the collar*)

No more 'my', brother. (*Goes.*)

WYAND: (*Stamping on the coin*) Uck you. (*Rounding on* **SYMOND**) And uck you, false prophet. Uck you, you funt. May you burn in ucking, funting hell, you uggerbay.

(*Goes.*)

SCENE SEVEN : THE WORD

(*The camp. Day.*
WILSE, YSOD)

YSOD: Two sentries, found with their throats cut.
WILSE: Then we must have more sentries, to guard the sentries.
YSOD: And yet more, to guard them?
WILSE: (*Irritated*) If need be, yes!
YSOD: Where does it end, this guarding.
WILSE: (*More patiently*) It doesn't. For he who guards my life becomes my brother.
YSOD: My brother's keeper, is it?
WILSE: Keeper, but not gaoler. There are no keys for a keeper of the house.

(*She starts to go out*)

YSOD: We need defences. Just adding men isn't enough.
WILSE: (*Stops and turns*) Would you have us live like some great lord, in a castle?
YSOD: They will send an army.
WILSE: Is it that, to keep out their army? Or to keep something else in?
// What has brought us here, all of us? A word. And that word has brought people together before: many, many times. It's a fine word, but it makes others jealous; too jealous. And so the people build a wall around the word to protect it, and that makes the others more jealous still, so jealous they want to knock it down. And then the wall has to be built higher and stronger, and the next thing you know it's a great house with a roof, and people come from all over to admire it, and be part of it, because it's so tall and strong; and soon it's become something far more grand, like a church, or a country. And after a while people start to forget about the word — because they're so busy, you see, so busy just building ... the mansion. And the word starts shrinking, because it needs light and air, and it's not getting any. And because it's so small it gets locked away in a backroom cupboard, and only gets brought out on special days, and then the days get less and less special, and no one cares about them any more except that they're a good excuse for a party. And one day the word just dies altogether and nobody notices, they're all too busy admiring the beautiful house.
//Some people would put a lid on the sky if they could get away with it.
YSOD: So live ... with no defences?
WILSE: Does not the sky go on forever? Let the sky of the brotherhood be our protection.

(*Goes.*
Pause/ **YSOD** *stands musing*)

YSOD: (*Shouts*) Yallop!

(**YALLOP** *enters*)

YALLOP: Yes, Captain?
YSOD: Brother. (*Walks away, comes back*) If we have God, do we need defences?
YALLOP: God, brother?
    // Some say that God made us to be like him, that God is someone we're all growing into. Brother Wyand says that God's a huge oak and we're the acorns, but we'll get there eventually.
YSOD: And what do you think.
YALLOP: I think we're a joke that's gone wrong, an afterthought. We were made last, after God had worn himself out making cats, stones, lizards, all those things without souls. When he made us he was getting sleepy and sentimental, like a tipsy uncle at a christening. So he allowed that little bit of feeling to creep in, the bit that's caused us all the trouble.
YSOD: So ... how do we get rid of it.
YALLOP: Turn the joke on him, pretend it never happened. Live like stones, brother.
YSOD: If we are already stones, do we need a wall around this Camp?
YALLOP: But we are not all stones, brother.

SCENE EIGHT: NIGHT, CITY

(*Night. A ruined church.*
Moon.
GRETA (*with bundle*), **SYMOND**)

GRETA: Why you following me like a dog? Bark, dog.
SYMOND: I'm not.
GRETA: Followed me to the bawdy house, nothing but a heap of old stones. Still didn't satisfy you. Had to follow me here as well. Heap of old stones number two. What'd you want?
SYMOND: What is this place?
GRETA: Never seen a church before? I used to come here and sit. Felt safe then. (*Looking around*) Nowhere to sit now.
SYMOND: I'd like to keep you safe. Again.
GRETA: Safe. Never clapped eyes on that for a long time. Seen plenty of the other. I seen dead babies and I seen them put in the ground. First one, then the next. Wanted to scrabble 'em out with my bare hands but Agnes said no, leave them, then Jesus'll know where they are on the Day of Judgement. You go carting them about, he'll never be able to find them.

(*He moves towards her*)

Don't want no more dead babies, boy.

(*Pause/there is a noise, off.*
MOW *comes in with pieces of stained glass in his hands*)

GRETA: Mow.
/ What you got there, Mow?
MOW: Jesus. Jesus house broken, look.

(*He puts the pieces of glass on the ground and tries to fit them together.*
GRETA *bends over him and sings softly, rocking the bundle*)

GRETA: (*Sings*)
        Sweet baby Jesus
        sat on a wall
        sweet baby Jesus
        had a great fall
        and all of Kett's horses
        and all of Kett's men
        couldn't put Jesus
        together again

(*She repeats the song,* **MOW** *joining in.*
At the end of the song she pats **MOW** *on the shoulder, then turns away from them both.*
MOW *continues to hum the song in snatches and play with the glass*)

GRETA: You got another she?
/ Whose place am I taking?
SYMOND: Why are you so sharp? I could cut myself just looking at you.
/ No one's place.
GRETA: One before, weren't there?

(*Pause*)

SYMOND: I want you to take your own place.
/ I want you to fill the space ... in me ... that's been waiting for you.

(*She cuddles the bundle closer to herself*)

GRETA: I don't want your kindness, boy, creeping in like a ghost where it's not wanted. Spoil everything, that do.

(*She turns to face him*)

I'm frightened, boy. Frightened of letting go and being nothing. You know what that's like?
// I had this ... it might have been a dream, I couldn't be sure. I couldn't get to sleep for the rain drumming on the thatch. Then I was in the ground under a layer of earth, and the rain was still falling. I could feel it pattering on my bones — no flesh, just bones. And then I weren't even that, I was just earth, and the rain was

still coming down. And then I floated away like water, flowed everywhere. I was a river, I reached everything — grass, and cows' udders, and little boys' pricks. And then I was the rain falling.

/ / Some nights I lay down to sleep I'd like to pull the sky over my head like a blanket. Feel safe then.

/ Did you ever feel safe?

SYMOND: At grandmother's. Grandfather had a bald head. Grandmother had fifty cats, all of them wild. At feeding time, it was like a tide of fur coming in. Meeows rising like sea spray. I used to crouch down behind a wall and watch them. And then the moon ...

GRETA: Was it the moon or your grandfather's bald head?

(*Pause*)

SYMOND: It was grandfather's head. It was too bright for the moon. It had blue veins on it, like rivers. Like a map of the moon.

/ Here. (*Holding out a ribbon*) To go with your black eyes.

GRETA: They're brown.

SYMOND: Don't you know everything's just another shade of black?

(*Pause*)

GRETA: (*To* MOW) Take them pictures back to the Camp, brother. Tha's too dark to see in here.

(*Pause/* MOW *goes*)

GRETA: (*Suddenly talking to the bundle*) What use is it, this? What can you do with it? Why does it have to come all at once, like a flood? Why can't you have it sprinkled a little each day, like salt?

(*A pause, then she holds out her hand for the ribbon*)

SYMOND: You need two hands. To put it on with.

(*Long pause, then she gently puts down the bundle*)

GRETA: You.

SYMOND: (*Looking at her*) Those eyes could wear away the stones in the street, the way the light does.

(*He ties the ribbon on her hair, then holds her.*
She looks over his shoulder, shivers)

SYMOND: What.

GRETA: Moon.

/ / Hold me boy, don't be gentle.

/ But tell me first. Tell me how tight you're going to hold me.

(*Pause*)

SYMOND: As tightly ... as your grave will hold you. As the earth will hold your bones.

SCENE NINE : NIGHT, FOREST

(*The camp. Night.*
A number of figures are seated around a fire. **SEVERAL** *is talking to a band of thieves —* **HUCK, CLOCK,** *and* **STARLING.** *A fourth thief,* **THE PRINCE OF MASTURBATORS,** *wears a long coat with pockets which are full of women's shoes; during the first half of the scene he takes them out carefully one by one and arranges them in a row in front of him, clutching himself as he does so, apparently oblivious of the others.* **JIG** *sits staring in dismay at his feet, which are encased in a new pair of ill-fitting boots. Apart sits* **AGNES,** *lost in herself*)

SEVERAL: What do you steal?
JIG: (*To no-one in particular*) I hate these boots.
CLOCK: Everything. You stop your cart to go for a piss — pouff — we steal the wheels.
HUCK: And not only that, brother Clock. (*To* **SEVERAL**) We steal the wheels off slow-moving carts.
STARLING: And not only that, brother Huck. (*To* **SEVERAL**) We steal the wheels off fast-moving carts.
CLOCK: And not only that.
        / You have a house? We take the straw from your walls and leave you only the mud. And the next time the wind blows — pouff — your house is blown down.
JIG: Pouff?
SEVERAL: What do you want with the straw?
HUCK: (*To* **CLOCK**) You should have taken the mud, fool.
CLOCK: (*Shrugs*) Sooner or later, everything is taken. We come back for the mud.
STARLING: We need the straw for the horse who belongs to the cart with no wheels. First we take the wheels, then the horse.
SEVERAL: That's putting the cart before the horse.
CLOCK: Just so.
JIG: I hate my feet even.
SEVERAL: Is there anything you can't steal?
CLOCK: Minutes. It takes a real thief to steal them, like a landowner or a judge. Everything else you can sell or bury.
JIG: I hate these boots, I said.
STARLING: Why?
JIG: Don't fit.
HUCK: You should learn to steal from people with bigger feet.
JIG: (*Attempting to take the boots off*) Can't you talk about something else?
SEVERAL: (*To* **CLOCK**) Don't you keep anything for yourself?
CLOCK: Nothing. Besides, where would we keep it? We live too much in fields,

out in the open. Even behind hedges, we can't get away with much. Now if we could steal a nice wall ...

HUCK: You should have taken the mud.

STARLING: (*To the* **PRINCE OF MASTURBATORS**) What do you say, Prince?

THE P OF M: (*Staring at the row of shoes*) Is this what it is?

HUCK: What is?

THE P OF M: (*Very fast, still staring at the row of shoes*) Before, we lived nowhere, we sheltered in ditches, at night we robbed travellers and spent the money on drink. And if we got caught, they hung us. Now, we live nowhere, we shelter under trees, there are no travellers to rob, and even if there were we couldn't rob them without a warrant from Kett, and if we do get a warrant from Kett, not that there's anyone to rob, we have to hand everything over as soon as we get back to the Camp, so there's nothing to spend on drink, and if we don't, they hang us.

/ Is this what it is?

(*Pause*)

JIG: (*Suddenly managing to get one boot off*) Blast these boots.

(*He hurls the boot into the night.*
There is a shout, off.
YALLOP *enters, holding the boot and rubbing his arm*)

YALLOP: Who threw this bollicking boot?

(*He looks around the company.*
JIG *attempts to hide his booted leg by tucking it underneath him*)

THE P OF M: (*Suddenly interested*) Is it a woman's boot?

YALLOP: (*Looking at the boot*) No brother, it is not.

STARLING: (*To* **YALLOP**) Are you hurt?

YALLOP: (*Still rubbing*) No, it's only a rumour. (*To* **JIG**) What's wrong with your leg?

JIG: Lost it brother, fighting against the Scots.

YALLOP: In whose company?

JIG: My Lord of Howard's, brother.

YALLOP: A company of thieves.

JIG: Just so, brother, just so. I was lucky to lose only my leg.

STARLING: (*To* **YALLOP**) Do you think they will send an army against us?

YALLOP: (*Ignoring her, to* **JIG**) You seem honest. Make it known that ... I seek the brother of this boot. (*Confidentially*) There's money in it. (*To the others*) Post the night watch, brothers. (*Goes off with the boot*)

CLOCK: (*To the* **PRINCE OF MASTURBATORS**) Come Prince, we have business with the night.

THE P OF M: Oh, the night, is it?

(**CLOCK** *and* **HUCK** *go out.*
THE PRINCE OF MASTURBATORS *scrabbles the shoes together and puts them back in his pockets.*)

THE P OF M: (*Going out, to* **STARLING**) Coming, brother? (*Goes.*)
STARLING: (*Doesn't answer*)
JIG: (*Taking off the other boot*) Where shall I hide this?
AGNES: (*Standing up*) Hide it in your face, it's where you hide everything else.

> (*She takes a blanket and settles herself for the night. Likewise* **JIG, SEVERAL,** *and* **STARLING. SEVERAL** *immediately falls asleep*)

JIG: Where's Greta?
AGNES: She'll be back.
STARLING: What's that noise?
AGNES: What noise. Do you want another blanket?

> (**STARLING** *shakes her head*)

It'll be the night, that's all.

> (*A pause, then* **MOW** *enters and stands in the darkness. They do not notice him until he speaks*)

MOW: Night.
STARLING: Mow.
JIG: Hey, Mow.

> (**MOW** *comes forward and examines his pieces of broken glass in the firelight.*)

STARLING: What you got?
MOW: Jesus. See — Jesus house broken. Greta said, take them pictures to the Camp, tha's too dark to see in here.
JIG: Where?
MOW: (*Patiently explaining*) Tha's too *dark*, Greta said.

> (*Pause*)

STARLING: This time o' day I always miss my cow. After I had milked her she would nuzzle my cheek. When I was sad I would put my arms around her neck: her big eyes would stare at me like moons.
MOW: Moon.
  / Jesus got a moon, see? Behind his head.

> (*Pause*)

STARLING: Do you think they will send an army against us?

> (*Long pause*)

AGNES: Look how the light still clings to the leaves, even at this hour. It won't let go of us, follows us everywhere.
  / And yet we never notice it in daytime.

(*Pause*)

STARLING: What *is* that noise?
JIG: Stones in the earth. Worms.
AGNES: What is that noise? It's just the night, the night and the forest rubbing together. They say the world has an edge like a plate, if you go too far out to sea you'll fall off it. But I don't think the edge is out to sea at all. I think it keeps moving around, sometimes it's far away and sometimes very close. Just now I think the edge is there, where the light stops. That's what that noise is: it's the night telling you there's things past there you don't know about.

/ Will they send an army? Of course they will.

/ / (*Suddenly irritated*) We live till we die. First day, then the night. What more do you want?

(*Pause*)

MOW: Worms.

SCENE TEN: THE HAWK

(*Camp. Morning.*
WYAND *is talking to* **SEVERAL**. *Nearby,* **JIG**)

WYAND: God sits on a cloud guarded by seven dragons. He sees everything, he hears everything.
JIG: (*To himself*) Mostly dragons' farts.
SEVERAL: Can he see us now?
WYAND: He sees everything.
SEVERAL: Can he see my fist?
WYAND: He sees everything.
JIG: The knife you keep under your cloak?

(*Pause*)

WYAND: He sees everything, brother.

(**GRETA** *and* **SYMOND** *come in.* **GRETA** *no longer has the bundle*)

JIG: Jack go a-rabbiting.

(**GRETA** *goes to fetch a cup of water from the bucket.*
SYMOND *is staring up at the sky*)

JIG: What you looking at?
SYMOND: Up there. A hawk.

(**YSOD** *enters*)

YSOD: A hawk, where?

SYMOND: There. Just a speck, scraping against the roof of the sky.

JIG: Probably a dragon.

WYAND: You blaspheme, you uggerbay. (*Goes*)

SYMOND: (*Still looking up*) What's it looking for?

YSOD: (*Suddenly grabbing* **SYMOND** *by the back of the neck*) Flesh, bone, scruff. The hawk's here. How'd you like the sky, says the hawk. (*Forcing his head up*) Blue? (*Pushing it down*) Gone. (*Forcing it up*) Grey? (*Pushing it down*) Gone. (*Forcing it up*) White fluffy bits? (*Pushing it down*) They've gone too. Which way round? (*Forcing it up*) Up? (*Pushing it down*) Down? Come on, you got to choose. (*Pushing him to the ground, face downwards*) Green? Brown? (*Kicking him in the face*) Red? Where's the sky gone?

(*He lets go of* **SYMOND**, *looks up*)

The hawk's gone too.

(**GRETA** *stands watching with a cup of water in her hand*)

GRETA: (*To* **YSOD**) No, it's still here.
/ Ever watched a hawk, I mean *really* watched it? It can see in the distance — it can see things like storms or little creatures on the floor of the forest, but if something comes right up to it, like this, suddenly, (*She comes right up to him*) you can't see it at all, can you?

(*Pause*)

YSOD: Come.

GRETA: You going to drag me brother, in front of the whole Camp?

(*Pause*)

YSOD: Never again (*Walking away, then stopping*) come close to me. And never once be alone with me. (*Goes*)

(**JIG** *stands up, begins to play a rollicking tune on the pipes.* **SEVERAL** *joins in with the words, alternating between two different voices,* **A** *and* **B**. *It becomes a 'performance', with both of them dancing around* **GRETA** *and* **SYMOND**.
SYMOND *remains on the ground, his face in his hands.*
GRETA *stands motionless, still holding the cup of water*)

SEVERAL: (*Sings*)

> **A:**   A face came laughing
> over the hill
> sweet face, pretty face
> dance where you will
> and what do you look for
> pretty-my-sweet?

B: "I look for another
to kill and eat."

A: But how will you kill him
face so dear
without any fingers
to strangle or tear?
B: "Oh I have my soft lips
and haven't you heard
I can kill very well
with a smile or a word."

B: "I don't need a body
or even an arm
when I've got my mouth open
I've lots of charm
so lay down beside me
and give me your heart
and once I've chewed on it
we never shall part."

(*Repeat, faster.*
SEVERAL *bows, then exits.*
JIG *plays the tune through once more, then dances out after him*)

GRETA: (*Bending down and cradling* **SYMOND**) Here boy, put your head in my lap, the cave of dead babies.

(*She gives him water.*)

SCENE ELEVEN : THE KING'S MESSENGER

(*A meeting is in progress. Amongst those present are* **SEVERAL, JIG, WILSE, YSOD, GRETA, AGNES, YAXLEY, STARLING, JACKER,** *and* **MOW.** *Facing them is* **THE KING'S MESSE NGER,** *wearing the costume of a herald. The first part of this scene (i.e. until* **WILSE** *speaks) should have an ever-increasing, reckless momentum, with lines being delivered at speed (and overlapping where indicated). There should be a strong sense that this is the most fearful, and yet most exciting, time of their lives — a time of danger, but also of delight*)

THE KING'S MESSENGER: (*Reading a proclamation*) If you now *leave this place* and now *cease this commotion* you shall be granted *the King's Pardon*. Which shall be extended to all here present *except those* who have urged on others in this wickedness, *namely: Robert Kett,* or Cat; one *Wilse,* called prophet; *Robert Ysod;* and all similar *Captains of Mischief,* who shall...

(*His words are drowned in an outburst of shouting*)

YSOD: But what of those *great lords of mischief*, the landowners?

STARLING: As soon as any man offend any of these gorgeous gentlemen he is put out, deprived, and thrust from all his goods.

YSOD: How long shall we suffer so great an oppression to go unrevenged?

AGNES: For so far are these gentlemen now gone in cruelty that not only do they take all by violence away from us, they must also *suck the blood and marrow out of our veins and bones.*

YAXLEY: The common pastures left by our fathers for our relief and our children (*Overlap* **STARLING**) are taken away.

STARLING: The lands which were common are hedged and ditched and made several, the pastures are enclosed (*Overlap* **JIG**) and we shut out.

JIG: The fowls of the air and fishes of the water and increase of the earth, these they do devour (*Overlap* **AGNES**) and swallow up.

AGNES: Yes, and nature alone cannot satisfy their lusts, but they must always be seeking out new devices with which to embalm and perfume themselves, to abound in pleasant smells and pour in sweet things to sweet things.

JACKER: While we must eat herbs and roots, and be kept in continual labour, and yet are envied that we live, breathe, and enjoy common air!

> (**SEVERAL** *begins beating his drum*)

YSOD: We would rather take arms, and *mix heaven and earth together*, than endure so great cruelty.

YAXLEY: We see that things have now come to extremities, and *we will prove the extremity.* We will rend down hedges, and fill up ditches, and make a way for everyman (*Overlap* **AGNES**) into the common pasture.

AGNES: And we will try all means, and not rest until we have brought things to our liking.

YSOD: We desire *liberty* and an equal use of all things. *This we will have. Otherwise these tumults and our lives shall only be ended together.*

> (*An outburst of cheering.*
> **SEVERAL** *brings his drumming to a crescendo, then stops.*
> *Whilst this is happening* **SYMOND** *slips in and stands next to* **GRETA**. *His face is swollen*)

MOW: (*To* **THE KING'S MESSENGER,** *as the cheering dies away*) And what d' you think of that?

> (*Laughter*)

THE KING'S MESSENGER: Are you then determined to be an army of rebels against the laws of this land?

> (*An outbreak of shouting*)

WILSE: (*Over this, to* **THE KING'S MESSENGER**) AND IS THAT NOT WHAT YOU WANT US TO BE, BROTHER?

(She waits for the last of the tumult to die away before she speaks again)

WILSE: (*To* **THE CROWD**) For they would love you to be an army, a rebels' army. An army they know. An army they can deal with. An army they can defeat.

/ For if you become an army, you will be defeated by an army. Would you become soldiers like them, to be cut down and killed?

/ An army is mere muscle, and blood; it is not a voice. An army can be in only one place; a voice can be in ten thousand different places — behind walls or hedges, or in the streets, or in the fields and woods. And you yourselves have seen it: a great city, the second city in the land, destroyed by *voices.*

JACKER: (*To the audience*) And I thought: perhaps we are only strong because we *are* together in one place. But I did not have the words, so I kept silent.

YAXLEY: (*To the audience*) And I thought of my fire, and I said: (*To* **WILSE**) was it not *fire* destroyed the city, brother?

WILSE: And was it not our breath that fanned the flames? (*To* **THE CROWD**) For we are here today as a brotherhood of *breath* — each breath joining to make a great wind that has rattled the gates of privilege and brought forth (*Indicates* **THE KING'S MESSENGER**) this gorgeous gentleman. And where you were once chained and shackled, you are now free — even as the wind is free. And what would you do with this wind? You would make of it ... an army. You would put a sword in its hand, and armour on its back. You would weigh down this great breath, this brotherhood, with ... things.

STARLING: (*To audience*) And I thought, I have felt the wind armed: at night, when I have lain in ditches, I have felt the wind armed with all manner of spikes, and stones, and mallets, to drive me from my sleep — but I was fearful of their laughter, and I kept silent.

JIG: (*To audience*) And I thought of our need for strength, to be strong against them, and I said: (*To* **WILSE**) you speak of an army of offence; do we not need an army of *de*fence, brother?

WILSE: Would you build a wall around this Camp? A wall, with watchtowers? As some great lord builds fences on his land? Is that not why we were driven to this, because of fences?

YAXLEY: (*To audience*) And I thought: a wall is easily attacked, we do not want a wall.

STARLING: (*To audience*) And then the fear came out of my mouth, and I said: (*To* **WILSE**) but whether we are an army or not, they will still send an army against us.

AGNES: How can they send an army against not an army?

(Laughter)

AGNES: (*To audience*) And I heard their laughter, and I grew more confident, and I said: (*To* **THE CROWD**) can we not learn to live in such a way that our lives are not the deaths of other people?

(Silence, then:)

YSOD: (*Charismatic and powerful*) But were we not brought here because of *death,* because we were worn down by *all those bitter deaths?* Deaths of the plough and the anvil, deaths on damp straw in the cold morning, deaths by the false axe in the forest, deaths of the sly ditch and the worm in the gut, deaths of the slow mud in the dark harbour — *and should we not give them back all these deaths?*

(*Shouting/* **SEVERAL** *drums*)

JACKER: (*As the shouting dies*) But must we spend all our strength attacking those who are rich and powerful?
YSOD: What is the point of attacking anyone else?

(*Silence*)

WILSE: Such hard deaths, these deaths of the plough and the harbour. But now we face others. Craftier, invisible. Deaths that will come as false friends, to whisper each day in our ears: how strong we are, perhaps . . *invulnerable.* Deaths that will enter our hearts when we gaze out from our watchtowers and imagine that the whole land bows down before us; or come as pride into our hands as we pull our sword from a man's neck, or aim our bows against a human target.
YAXLEY: (*To audience*) And I thought of a line of fat stomachs, and me with a hundred arrows, and I thought, yes, I would like to feel that.
WILSE: How tempting it is, brothers, to turn your pain, your hunger, all these little deaths, into hatred. But this hatred will kill you more surely than the deaths of the plough and the harbour; for these kill only your body, whilst the hatred will kill your spirit, make you kill your true self and build the false one in its place.
AGNES: (*To audience*) And I felt that pain, that hunger, at the ends of my fingers — just itching for a white neck or to get out into the air, and I said: (*To* **WILSE**) then what shall we do with it, this pain?
WILSE: Cherish it: as opportunity. And use the strength it gives us, not against others, but against...ourselves.
JACKER: (*To audience*) And I thought: they call her a prophet, I will listen to her. I do not understand, but I will listen to her.
WILSE: What is our greatest possession in this Camp? Not guns, or swords, or sheepskins, but just this, what we are doing now: talking. That is our most important task: to talk, to change ourselves; to cast off old pain, old hunger, and become truly free. To become ... ourselves. And can we do that by shouting at some gentleman in a gorgeous coat?
MOW: (*To* **THE KING'S MESSENGER**) And what d'you think of that?

(*Silence*)
WILSE: We make our enemy. He could not exist without us, for we make him out of all our hatreds, deep inside ourselves. All that we cannot face in us, we face in him. Is that who we want to kill, brothers? Do we want to kill ... ourselves?

(*Muttering among* **THE CROWD**)

YAXLEY: (*To audience*) And I thought: what am I then to attack? That within me, or that without? At least give me something. I must have something to fight against, brother.
AGNES: (*To audience*) And I thought: we stand here like sheaves of corn, like beasts in a field. We know nothing. And after you have said this, we still know nothing.

STARLING: (*To audience*) And I thought: I do not know what to think. I will go away, and think more on this. And then Ysod spoke.

YSOD: But brother Wilse is right: our pain *is* opportunity, and we must cherish it. For what do we fight against? Lies, greed, and privilege. And to fight them we need the most powerful weapons. And we have those weapons here: lies, greed, and privilege — the same. Because to *hate* these things gives us the strength to fight against them. To hate, brothers. Hold fast to your hatred. It is a most precious thing.

YAXLEY: But what does Kett say?

VOICES: Kett! Kett!

YSOD: Kett goes by the will of the Camp. Kett says: *whatever you say yourselves.* Kett says: that his world, (*Points to* **THE MESSENGER**) the world that judges some men as more important than others, *is a lie.* Kett says, that only one thing is important: *that no one is less important.*

DIFFERENT VOICES: Kett! Kett!
> Death to the Messenger!
> Put him in the stocks!

> (**THE KING'S MESSENGER** *makes a signal to someone behind him — a downward sweep of the hand.* **JIG** *and* **YAXLEY** *rush out and bring in the stocks (from Scene Two).*
> *General tumult, in the midst of which* **THE KING'S MESSSENGER** *quietly exits unnoticed*)

WILSE: (*Attempting to intervene*) Is this not a master's punishment? Take them away. We have no masters here.

> (*Uncertainty amongst* **THE CROWD**)

GRETA: He's gone anyway. (*Pointing*) Look, he's getting on his horse.

MOW: (*Shouting after* **THE MESSENGER**) Why don't you, why don't you, (*It finally comes out in a rush*) why don't you get off and milk it!

> (*Laughter and cheering*)

YSOD: Take the stocks away, brothers.

> (**THE CROWD** *disperses in good humour, taking the stocks with them.*
> *Three people are left:* **WILSE, YSOD,** *and (standing apart from them)* **SEVERAL**)

YSOD: (*To* **WILSE**) And when they come, brother, will you be standing as an oak in the line?

> (**WILSE** *looks at* **YSOD**, *doesn't answer; exits.*
> **YSOD** *watches her go, then exits in the other direction*)

SEVERAL: (*Taking out a model of his own head on a stick and speaking to it*) All revolution against the status quo is reactionary because it defines itself in reaction's terms, albeit as an opposite. True revolution will arise from nothing. It will require nothing to feed it. It will be completely stupid.

SCENE TWELVE : ANGELS

(*Camp.*
AGNES, GRETA.
Both are engaged in camp business — sorting firewood into piles — which continues at intervals throughout the scene)

AGNES: What do you know about him.
GRETA: What he's told me. That's enough.
AGNES: Enough. There's no such thing. Not even *enough* is enough.

(*Pause*)

GRETA: We're blood.
AGNES: Blood.
/ Blood only mixes with blood when it's spilt on the same patch of ground.
/ / (*She takes a step towards* **GRETA**) Look ...
GRETA: (*Turning away*) Don't breathe on me.
AGNES: Oh my life.
/ You come here ...
GRETA: I didn't come. I was brought.
AGNES: What brought you?
GRETA: (*Doesn't answer*)
AGNES: I'll tell you: the way you walk. Like you got a gold piece stuck up your arse and you're trying to get it out without the aid of your hands. That's what brought you.
GRETA: You talking to me or chewing a brick? You're dust. Your mouth is just dust.
AGNES: Oh my life. You got fruit on the outside but the stone in the centre is hard.

(*Pause*)

GRETA: (*Suddenly walking right up to* **AGNES**, *vicious*) I don't see no dancing bears. I don't see no tumblers. I don't see no dogs jumping through hoops. I don't see no dark lady telling fortunes. In fact I don't see no fairground at all. So what you doing here, *clown*?

(**AGNES** *is not intimidated.*
GRETA *walks away*)

GRETA: (*Stands facing away from* **AGNES**) What d'you want from me.
AGNES: Not to be a fool.
GRETA: I've tried everything else. (*She turns around*) Sometimes I think all I want is to love somebody so much I don't know where I stop and they begin. But instead

of that it's like I've rolled on top of something and crushed it. Like when you're laying on the grass and you roll over and it could be a tiny animal, anything. And you stand up and brush yourself and start to look for it, try to see what it is you've rolled on top of. But there's nothing there. You look and look but you can't never find it.

/ What d'you think *he* wants from me.

AGNES: What any man wants, to keep from falling.

/ Ever noticed how our body's a dead end? In here? Like a bag. Ever been called that? *"You old bag"*. But the bag's necessary, you see — otherwise they'd push in and fall straight through us, end up in space somewhere.

// To be stopped from falling, that's what they want. And what they don't want.

(*Pause*)

GRETA: I want to make it special, like Christmas. That's all.

(*Pause*)

AGNES: Special.

/ When I was a girl I went out one Christmas Eve to look for angels. Searched the whole damn heavens. Not a sign of them. Everyone was saying "It's Christmas, it's Christmas", and singing songs about angels and bright lights in the sky. But all I could see were the same stars I saw every night through the holes in our roof. And then I realised: the angels don't just come out at Christmas, they're there all the time. But for one night a year we have to call them angels, and that's what makes the rest of the year seem dark.

// You don't have to make it anything. Do you?

(*A pause, then* **GRETA** *starts to furiously sort the firewood.*
AGNES *watches her for a few moments, then goes up to her, puts her hand on* **GRETA's** *arm.*
GRETA *stops*)

AGNES: Hold on to it.

// We can't love enough. So we do all these other things. But it's all instead of love, really. Everything's frustrated love. Everything.

SCENE THIRTEEN[2] : 'I'

(*Camp.*
WILSE, SYMOND)

SYMOND: (*Restless*) Why is everything so difficult?
WILSE: What is? The sky does not find things difficult, neither does the earth.

---

[2]   See appendix.

SYMOND: I am not the sky or the earth.
WILSE: Oh — I, is it? But does this I not touch them? Look.

(*She draws the shape of an 'I' on the ground.*)

I

Here is your I. Long and narrow, with a roof for the sky and two feet for the earth. See how thin it is, this I of yours — almost invisible. And yet joined to everything. But now see what happens. The I is not satisfied with earth and sky, it has to grow fat of itself, look — see how your name adds to its volume.

(*She adds to the drawing:*)

SYMOND

And as you grow older, the I grows more and more. You were a ...

(*She adds to the drawing:*)

And then an ...

(*She adds to the drawing:*)

What next. Perhaps a …

(*She adds to the drawing:*)

Or even a …

(*Adds to the drawing:*)

See how the poor I is pulled this way and that. So important, so heavy — and yet the true I is lost. Now.

(*She scrubs out the drawing and starts again. Draws:*)

$$I \quad \overset{I}{\underset{I}{}} \quad \underset{I}{\overset{I}{}} \quad \overset{I}{\underset{I}{}} \quad \underset{I}{\overset{I}{}} \quad \overset{I}{\underset{I}{}}$$

You and your brothers. What do they most resemble?

(**SYMOND** *puzzles over it.* **WILSE** *adds:*)

SYMOND: The rain, that falls between sky and earth.
WILSE: Just so. And each drop unique, a clear crystal. But look.

(*She adds a number of connecting words, obscuring the 'I's, eg:*)

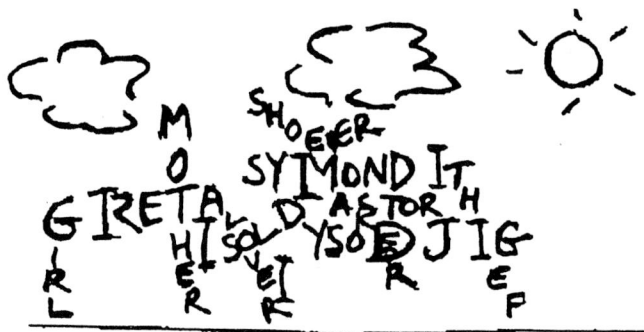

The I's are lost and scream for attention. Even in the brightest day, there is a great darkness because of the jumble of I's.

(**SYMOND** *walks away, thinking*)

SYMOND: (*Turns and comes back*) But is there not a great comfort in this darkness, a comfort in knowing that the I is not alone, and all others are similarly dark?
WILSE: It is true, there is a great and false comfort.
SYMOND: But the true I, the I that lives in the light, is this not to be terribly alone?

(*Pause*)

WILSE: Think of the rain, brother: I's like rods of water. Like rods of rain falling.

SCENE FOURTEEN : THE BANQUET IN THE FIELD

(A field near the camp. Sunset.
AGNES, MOW, JIG, SEVERAL, HOWLING, GRETA, SYMOND, STARLING, JACKER, YAXLEY.
During the first part of the scene, a number of objects are brought in and arranged haphazardly in the centre of the playing area. These include: a long table, assorted chairs, a white tablecloth, items of food and drink, cutlery, silverware, etc)

JACKER: *(As more objects are brought in)* Is there yet more?
YAXLEY: *(Entering with drink)* And yet more after this, brother.
SYMOND: But why have they fled?
SEVERAL: Because they fear us. It is a simple thing, fear.
HOWLING: From King's Lynn to Yarmouth, and south to Diss so they say, nothing but great houses abandoned to the elements.
SYMOND: But why ...
SEVERAL: *It is a simple thing, fear.*

(More objects are brought in.
A number of people are now seated around the table, eating and drinking.
SYMOND *goes out)*

JACKER: Why are we eating out here, when there's a perfectly good ...
JIG: Old ways, brother. Let our room be empty, with the wind blowing through. As brother Wilse said.
YAXLEY: *(To himself)* Wilse.
GRETA: *(Looking around)* But if someone comes, there's nowhere to knock.
SEVERAL: *(Eating)* Good. Nowhere to knock is good.
STARLING: *(Arranging spoons in a row in front of her)* Soldiers.
YAXLEY: Fire the house, I say. Fire all their houses.
JACKER: Wilse said not to. Pass us that drink.

*(**MOW** is examining his reflection in a silver plate)*

MOW: *(To* **HOWLING***)* 'S my face, see? Agnes said so. Got my face on a plate.
HOWLING: Let's have a look.

(He takes the plate from **MOW***, looks at it)*

That's not your face, it's mine.
MOW: *(Snatching it back)* Not your face! My face!

(He holds the plate up to his face for the rest of the scene)

AGNES: *(To herself)* It is mad to be so full of things. *(Suddenly, to the others)* Is this not what madness is, to be so full of things? Like the madman in the market-place who is so full of words, full to over-bursting?

JIG: (*Patting himself contentedly*) My stomach is mad. My stomach is the very maddest of stomachs.

AGNES: (*Reaching over to push the spoons away from* **STARLING**, *knocking over a glass of wine as she does so*) Don't fill your empty room with *things*, brother Wilse said.

YAXLEY: Wilse this, Wilse that.

JIG: Wilse the other.

YAXLEY: (*Rounding on* **JIG**) The other what? The other life, that is richer than this life? (*Standing up, angrily*) What shines on Wilse? The other sun, that is brighter than this sun? What rains on Wilse? The other rain, that is gentler than our rain? What protects Wilse? (*Picking up a knife*) The other knife, that is sharper than this knife? *What is it with Wilse?* Don't she shit out of the same hole as the rest of us? Why, she will soon be a new god, this Wilse.

(*Pause*)

SEVERAL: (*Taking out his head on a stick and talking to it*) Mark Chapter Seven: evil cometh not from without, but from within, saith the Lord. (*To* **YAXLEY**) Sit down, brother.

> (**YAXLEY** *sits down, unsteadily.*
> **SYMOND** *comes in with a pane of glass*)

SYMOND: Look, Greta. It's what they put in their wind-holes to keep out the rain and cold.

JACKER: (*To herself*) Glass.

GRETA: And let in the light.

SYMOND: And let in the light, yes.

> (*He holds up the glass between them. She looks through it, frowning. Then presses her lips against it. His lips meet hers on the other side of the glass. He takes the glass away, holds her*)

YAXLEY: (*Drinking*) It was Kett I meant, not Wilse.

> (**JIG** *begins to play a slow lament on his pipes*)

SEVERAL: (*Sings*)
> She was wet to my touch
> like a rain-soaked field
> but her heart was a box
> I could not find it
>
> The air was warm
> and the night ran on
> while that sweet earth turned
> in my open hand

And the earth was wet
to my touch, to my touch
but her heart was a box
I could not find it

(*As* **JIG** *plays the tune through once more,* **YSOD** *enters with a sword in his hand.*
He stands in the growing darkness, watching them. They do not notice him.
And then the sword is thrown to land with a crash on top of the table.
They freeze)

YSOD: (*Coming forward*) Come, brothers. My Lord of Northampton's army is outside the city. Now is the time for fighting.

(**MOW** *is the only one to move: he slowly lowers the plate from his face and goes to*
put it under his shirt)

YSOD: (*Stopping him*) No, brother. Danger is lightness.

(*A sudden gust of wind.*
Lights fade to black.
INTERMISSION)

SCENE FIFTEEN: TAKE ARMS FOR PEACE

(*The camp.*
A celebration is in progress — dancing, music. Amongst the crowd are **AGNES,**
GRETA, YALLOP, STARLING, JACKER, YAXLEY, MOW, WILSE,
and **YSOD.**
To one side is **SEVERAL,** *talking to* **SYMOND** *and* **JIG.** *Near them, a circle of*
powder has been sprinkled to represent 'the world'; the action of the 'play within a
play' will take place inside this. Nearby, a small tent or curtained-off area which will
be used as a changing room. **SEVERAL** *wears a voluminous black cloak and carries*
a sack; he moves awkwardly. **SYMOND** *and* **JIG** *are dressed as normal.*)

SEVERAL: Have you your parts?

(**SYMOND** *nods*)

JIG: Have I my own hand, my foot?
SEVERAL: Then to it.

(**SYMOND** *and* **JIG** *go into the tent*)

The two of them totalled may yet make one actor.

(*He beats on his drum. The music and dancing come to a gradual stop as the*
crowd gathers round him)

SEVERAL: And now: as *celebration* of this great *victory* (*Cheers from* **THE CROWD**) over my Lord of Northampton (*Jeers, boos*) and his lieutenant the Lord Sheffield ... *deceased* (*Cheers*) we offer for your special delight a most daring and instructive interlude, entitled ...

/ *entitled...*

VOICE FROM THE TENT: Take Arms for Peace.

SEVERAL: Take Arms for Peace, my masters.

> (*Drumroll.*
> **SYMOND** *and* **JIG** *come out of the tent.* **SYMOND** *wears a helmet;* **JIG** *is dressed as a girl, wearing a long wig and the tablecloth from Scene Fourteen, which is wrapped around him as a dress.* **JIG** *goes to recline at the rear of the circle;* **SYMOND** *takes up a position on the opposite side of it, next to* **SEVERAL**. **THE CROWD** *is noisy at first, but gradually falls silent as the play progresses.*)

MOW: Is that a man or a woman?

YAXLEY: Neither.

MOW: What?

STARLING: Be quiet.

SEVERAL: (*Points to the circle*) Behold: the world.
　　This pretty maid (*Points to* **JIG**) is *Peace*,
　　this slender youth (*Points to* **SYMOND**) is *Hope*.

YAXLEY: And who are you?

SEVERAL: My name (*Reaches into the sack, brings out a horrific mask*) is *War*.

> (*A murmuring in* **THE CROWD**.
> **WAR** *puts on the mask and stands in the centre of the circle, between* **PEACE** *and* **HOPE**)

HOPE: I am in love (*Points to* **PEACE**) with this fair maid.
　　Her gentle ways shall soothe my life.
　　(*Sees* **WAR**) But who is this?

MOW: War.

STARLING: Quiet.

HOPE: I cannot see my love — he blocks the way.

WAR: (*To* **HOPE**) Come, buy.

HOPE: What do you sell?

WAR: (*Taking out the contents of his sack*) These heads.

> (*A shudder runs through* **THE CROWD**)

HOPE: (*After a pause*) What is your price?

WAR: Your own. Your head for these.

HOPE: (*After a pause*) But — why?

WAR: No why. My name is War: my trade is heads.
　　Come, buy. If you'd see Peace again,
　　then buy my heads.

HOPE: And lose my own? No thanks.

WAR: (*Taking a sword from under his cloak*) Then fight.

HOPE: I am unarmed.
WAR: If you'd win Peace, then fight.
    Or else: give me your head.
HOPE: (*After a pause*) I'll fight.

    (*A cheer from* **THE CROWD**.
    HOPE *and* **WAR** *grapple with each other — it should be a stylised, slow-motion contest.* **WAR** *gives* **HOPE** *a blow with his sword, then drops it. As soon as* **HOPE** *is hit,* **PEACE** *stands up, clutching her heart.*)

PEACE: I bleed.

    (*A red stain appears on her breast.*
    There is a gasp from the crowd)

MOW: Peace bleeds! Peace bleeds!

    (**HOPE** *picks up the sword and deals* **WAR** *a deadly blow.*)

WAR : (*Sinks down*) I die. (*Dies*)
HOPE : (*Taking the sack*) I'll take these heads.
PEACE : (*Holding out her arms*) Sweet Hope,
    you were so brave. Come, rest here in my arms.

    (*She kneels down and takes him in her arms. He immediately falls asleep, his head on her breast*)

    And now this youth is fast asleep
    I'll take these heads and bury them,
    so they might rest.

    (*She tries to take the sack of heads which HOPE is still holding*)

HOPE : (*As if dreaming*) My heads!
    Someone would steal my heads! Die, thief!

    (*He stabs* **PEACE** *in the breast with the sword.*
    PEACE *dies immediately.*
    HOPE *wakes to find* **WAR** *rising from the dead.*)

WAR: Now Peace is dead, I rise again.
    I claim my heads.

    (*He throws his black cloak over* **PEACE,** *who disappears. Under the cloak* **WAR** *is wearing a straw costume, and a second sword*)

CRIES FROM THE CROWD: The Straw Man! The Straw Man!
HOPE: (*Searching about*) My Peace is gone!
    Where is my Peace?

(*He comes face to face with* **WAR**)

WAR: You'll have no Peace whilst I am in the world.

(*He strikes* **HOPE** *on the top of the helmet, knocking him back to the edge of the circle*)

    If you'd have Peace,
    then first you must have War.
HOPE: But still I have one weapon left:
    to find my Peace, *I'll burn you*, man of straw,
    I'll burn you from the world.

(*He sets light to the powder, creating a circle of fire. Then advances on* **WAR**, *a flame in his hand*)

    To find my peace I'll deal in *flames*,
    and never rest until I drive
    your darkness from the earth.

WAR : To save the world you'd burn the world.
    The world is now in flames.

(*Sudden blackout — all that can be seen is the circle of fire.*
When lights fade up, **SEVERAL**, **JIG**, *and* **SYMOND** *are standing together in the centre of the circle, surrounded by flames.* **JIG** *begins playing a tune on his pipes. During the ensuing song,* **SEVERAL** *uses various props (a handful of earth, some water, a flaming stick etc.) which are handed to him by* **SYMOND**)

SEVERAL : (*Sings*)
    1.   Oh come with me now
         said my lord of the sky
         and I'll show you the world
         from my kingdom on high
         you'll rule all the earth
         and you'll rule all the sea
         but until you have fire
         you'll never rule me

    2.   Oh come with me now
         said my lord of the waves
         and follow the fish
         as they spawn in their caves
         and once you have tasted
         my waters so warm
         you'll forget all that ails you
         and dance until dawn

3. Oh come with me now
said my lord of the earth
you must cling to my body
till you know what it's worth
and if you work hard
till the day that you're dead
I'll let you sleep soundly
in my wormy bed

(**SYMOND** *begins beating the drum*)

4. Oh come with me now
said my lord of the fire
and live in my flames
as they burn higher and higher
for I have the power
to burn earth and sea
and we'll fill all the sky
till it holds only me

(*Repeat last four lines,* **SYMOND** *joining in.*
They take their bows.
SEVERAL *begins putting out the flames,* **JIG** *and* **SYMOND** *tidy up the effects.*
THE CROWD *disperses.*
JIG *notices* **YALLOP** *in the crowd and starts to hop on one (the wrong) leg)*

YSOD: (*Going up to* **SEVERAL**) Who invented this.
SEVERAL: No invention, Captain — it was a thing of air. We merely reached up our hands, (*Gesture*) and down it came.

(**YSOD** *looks at him, says nothing, goes*)

YALLOP: (*Going up to* **JIG**) A miracle.
JIG: What is, brother?
YALLOP: The leg you lost to the Scots has been returned to you. And yet (*Looking down*) now it seems that you have lost its twin.
JIG: Just so, brother.
 / Sheer carelessness.

(**YALLOP** *stares at him, starts to move away, then stops*)

YALLOP: (*Not looking at* **JIG**) What has ten thousand heads and its tail between its legs?
JIG: Northampton's army.
YALLOP: What has two legs but no head and lies in a ditch?
JIG: The Lord Sheffield.
YALLOP: Where is Sheffield's head?
JIG: (*Doesn't answer*)

YALLOP: (*Turns to look at him*) *Where is Sheffield's head?*
JIG: (*Doesn't answer*)

> (**YALLOP** *goes up to him, holds him by the throat*)

YALLOP: Sheffield's head ... (*Laughs suddenly*) ... is with your leg ... and the rest of my hand.

> (*Holds up his other hand, which is now bloody, with fingers missing. Laughs again, louder. Takes his hand from* **JIG's** *throat*)

It was a good ... performance, brother.

> (*Goes out, still laughing.*
> **JIG** *watches him go, then cautiously lowers his leg to the ground.*)

SCENE SIXTEEN: THE HOUSE IN THE FOREST

> (*Towards evening. Another part of the forest.*
> **SYMOND** *is building a shelter with leaves and branches. Nearby is* **GRETA,** *only half listening to him*)

SYMOND: (*At the entrance to the shelter*) I want to step across and feel it: the new life. Like a line on the grass only you can't see it. Like a door, only you don't have to open it. And on the other side: the new life.
/ (*Low*) It's impossible.
/ I want somewhere to put the special things. (*To* **GRETA**) You know, the special things everyone has. (*Back to his work*) If you don't have somewhere to put them, the special things don't come to you.
GRETA: (*To herself*) Everything's changed, even my tongue. It used to be flint, but now it's a worm — just a worm in my jaw. (*To* **SYMOND**) Do you know what I mean?

> (*He doesn't answer, carries on building*)

Come closer.
SYMOND: I want to build this.
GRETA: Do you not find me sweet any more?
SYMOND: I just want to build *this*.

> (*Pause*)

GRETA: Do you not find me sweet any more, brother?
SYMOND: (*Stopping work*) Is the world sweet?

/ I no longer find the world sweet, and you are part of the world.
GRETA: But I am not, brother.
SYMOND: How is that.
GRETA: I am part of the world and I am not, brother. For here I am talking to you, and I am part of the world. And yet there is something in me that is not here talking to you, and is not part of the world. And is that not the part you find most sweet, brother?

(*Pause/he looks at her as if for the first time*)

SYMOND: (*Tries to take her in his arms*) Come ...
GRETA: (*Turning away*) And do you think you can find it by taking me in your arms, brother?

(*Pause*)

SYMOND: Why do you turn away?
/ Why do you ...
GRETA: (*Suddenly angry*) What you want me to do, bring it here and keep it all in the one place? And here is a door for it and here is a roof? What you going to do with it, pet it and coax it and let it out through a hole in the roof, like smoke? (*Straight in his face*) Fire, boy. There's only two things you can do with that: put it out and have done with it, or let it burn. *You can't be kind to it.* (*She turns away*)

(*Pause*)

SYMOND: It would have to be a house of nothing then, for you to live in it.
GRETA: (*Less angry*) How is that.
SYMOND: Why else your flames would burn the house up. And then it would be nothing, even though it had once been something.
GRETA: But if it were built of nothing, how would it then stand?
SYMOND: Perhaps not a house, perhaps a room only. For does the book not say that within the one mansion there are many rooms?
GRETA: Many rooms yes, but many rooms of nothing, I have not heard that.
SYMOND: But just one room. Could that not be built, do you think?

(*Pause/he rests his foot against the shelter and looks at it.*
THE LEPER *comes in.*)

THE LEPER: Would you be needing that little house, sir, lady?
SYMOND: What?
THE LEPER: Would you be needing that little house? I had one like it until yesterday, outside the walls it was, outside the big little city it was.
GRETA: I seen it, a leper house.
THE LEPER: Outside the walls it was, and then the battle came, and with the battle the fire came, and the blaze came over the wall and turned my house to ash. Outside the walls it was, outside the big little city it was.
SYMOND: Big little?

THE LEPER: Big sir, because it is fair and stretches greatly upon the earth. But close your eyes and you are in a different world, where only the things of the heart may live. And then is it not small indeed?

(*Pause*)

GRETA: What do you want?
THE LEPER: To live, lady — simply that. As the birds do, or the beasts of the field.

(*Pause*)

SYMOND: Do you need straw? We will bring you straw. (*To* **GRETA**) Come.

(**SYMOND** *and* **GRETA** *go out, leaving* **THE LEPER**)

SCENE SEVENTEEN: BLOOD ON THE STRAW

(*Morning.*
Forest, same location as previous scene.
At the entrance to the shelter is a heap of straw. Off, the sound of hammering.
WILSE, YSOD)

WILSE: What is that hammering?
YSOD: Defences.

(**WILSE** *looks at him*)

We have defeated one army. An army led by a fool. They will send another. Not led by a fool.
WILSE: (*Looking at the shelter*) What is this?
YSOD: (*Shrugs*)
/ And when they come, we let them into the city — we can't defend six miles of walls. And then: they are in the city, and we are up here, on the high ground.
/ But ...
WILSE: There is a but?
YSOD: With the city goes the food. And we are sixteen thousand. In three days they will throw a noose around this hill and we shall starve. We have to lure them to battle, before hunger comes.
WILSE: How?
YSOD: Leave this place. Fire it. Take with us our stakes, our defences. They will see the smoke, and follow us.
/ And so we shall meet them. On open ground.

(*Pause*)

WILSE: How long can they keep an army here? One month? Two? With the Scots nibbling at their throat and the French at their arse?
YSOD: Meanwhile we starve. Hunger is their best weapon.
WILSE: There is another way.

(**YSOD** *looks at her*)

Disperse. Be what we were before: scattered. Refuse to work for them. Plunder, live off the land. Not as one body, with sixteen thousand mouths to feed — but in two's and three's, separately.
YSOD: A hole to stop the wind.
        / They would hunt us down. Hunt us down and kill us.
WILSE: We would be *scattered* — in hedgerows, and ditches.
        / You would rather lead us to our deaths.
YSOD: I follow orders.
        / He says, there is no other way. (*Looking at* **WILSE**) Are you afraid?
WILSE: Yes. Are you?
YSOD: (*Doesn't answer*)

(*There is a rustling in the straw*)

WILSE: What is that in the straw?

(**YSOD** *puts his hand in*)

YSOD: Aaah! It bites! (*Stabbing the straw*) A rat! A rat in the straw!

(*He uncovers the straw and discovers* **THE LEPER**)

WILSE: Who is this poor creature?

(*Pause*)

YSOD: (*Shouts*) Yallop!

(**YALLOP** *enters*)

YALLOP: Captain?
YSOD: Burn this — and its house with it.
YALLOP: Captain. (*Goes*)

(**WILSE** *covers* **THE LEPER's** *body with straw*)

YSOD: (*Takes off his glove, examines his hand*)All those who would oppose me, let them walk the earth: it is myself I see in their battle-line. But this other ...
WILSE: Give me your glove.

(**YSOD** *gives it to her*, **WILSE** *puts it on*)

Fear. (*Holding up her gloved hand*) Is this not where we carry it? Here, at the very edge of us. And always we are seeking to pass it on: (*Demonstrates on* **YSOD**) with a blow, or a handshake. So many hard hands, so many brave commanders. All wearing the glove of our fear. And always (*Demonstrates by shaking hands with* **YSOD**) it comes back to us.

(*She takes off the glove*)

It is not fear's glove we should be wearing, but the great glove of the world.

(**YSOD** *stares at her*)

Do you not see? It surrounds us all the time, like a great empty glove: the *miraculous*. And all we have to do (*Demonstrates with her bare hand*) is put our hand in.
  / Can we not do this — cast off the glove of our fear and simply live...as flesh?
YSOD: (*Taking the glove back*) There are times when I would *smash* the world, smash it into little pieces, for the things it has done to me.
WILSE: But you would still be one of the little pieces.
  / And you would hold on to that piece, hold on like death, whilst you watched everything else fall and shatter. But we can only live — *truly* live — broken. Only by living broken can we hope to die whole.
YSOD: (*Quietly*) May I live whole, though I die broken.
WILSE: And is this not your refuge, this wholeness? Whilst you maim and burn and slaughter — will there not always be a part of yourself you return to and admire, like a jewel in a secret room? Oh, you've let go of all the other refuges — money, possessions. You've even let go of what most people use — another human being. But you'll never let go of that precious jewel of *yourself*.
YSOD: Precious. Yes, I am precious. And it is not the jewel, it is the very room. A room that has been built by racks, and cold, and hunger. And I would not wish it a minute less, any of it — because each minute made me *more precious still*. They have built my resistance until it is a *fortress*. It is our strongest weapon, this preciousness. Theirs is hunger. *Ours is this*.
WILSE: But it is a serpent. (*Going right up to* **YSOD**)For do you not see how *this*, (*Striking him on the chest*) this thing inside, would swallow you for its own use? Those lily smiles, the fear in their eyes when they look at you - all these it will take, and make them stones and bricks, and build of them.
  /And all things else - all that it cannot use - it has to push away: with rage, and distancing. It only loves what it can feed upon; its only god is ownership. But ownership is death. Once let it in, and ownership is all. For everything it sees, it turns into itself. Or into...other.
  // And other it hates. All that is not itself, it hates. It would set a moat between you and the world, and make the world your enemy. And it loves the battle, for battle makes it strong. Without battle, it is nothing.
  // If you'd be free, then rid yourself of this: all that which makes you special to yourself. All that pain, all that persecution. Seek out the proudest, most secret

part of yourself, that place you keep as refuge from the world, and kill it. Completely and forever. Burn down your house.

(*Pause /***YSOD** *turns away*)

YSOD: Everywhere you look there's this terrible love. Sweet and sticky, covering everything. Like a monster, sucking you in. So you're looking out through *its* eyes, thinking *its* thoughts. And you know the only way to escape is to kill it. When it's not looking. With a knife, from the inside.
  / And then you're free, free for the first time. But it's an awful freedom, the freedom of the last man on earth. It eats into you, that freedom, it changes the bones of your face. And there's only one thing can cure it, so you go looking for it again: that terrible love.
  / / (*Turns to face her*) I have no house.
WILSE: You must burn down the house you have built in your heart. Burn everything, right to the smallest, most secret room. Before you yourself become brick. Burn it until there is nothing left, not even ashes. Not even the dust of ashes.

(*A pause, then ***SYMOND** *and* **GRETA** *come in.* **SYMOND** *carries a bucket of water*)

SYMOND: (*Going up to the shelter*) Brought you some water. You there?

(*He stares at the pile of straw*)

GRETA: There's blood on the straw, look.

(**YALLOP** *enters with a flaming torch and stands watching them*)

WILSE: If blood and fire come in the morning, what shall be here by nightfall.

(*A pause, then* **YALLOP** *starts towards the shelter*)

YSOD: (*To* **YALLOP**) Leave that. (*Pointing at* **WILSE**) Arrest this woman and take her to the Oak.

(**YALLOP** *throws the torch into* **SYMOND's** *bucket, extinguishing it*)

YALLOP: (*To* **WILSE**) Come, brother.
WILSE: What is the charge.

(*Pause/***YSOD** *makes one of his hands into a fist*)

YSOD: Of nothing. (*Slowly unclenching it*) Let the charge be … of nothing.

(**YALLOP** *takes* **WILSE** *out*)

SCENE EIGHTEEN : CLOTHES, RIVER, EARTH

(*River bank. Early afternoon.*
AGNES, GRETA, JACKER, *and* **STARLING** *are washing clothes. Nearby, a spade*)

AGNES: (*Stops work*) See how we all go to our deaths. And they say, do not talk about this.

/ Suppose, when you were out walking, a big thing would come and knock you down. Perhaps even a small thing.

/ Some deaths hide behind walls. They take things quickly, even a smile. We go towards them as if pulled on a string. Laughing or silent, it is all the same.

/ I had a friend in a high place. Her death came swift ...

(*She is upset. She waits to recover herself*)

/ / / I had a friend in a high place. Her death came swift in the afternoon. In the pit of night, when the sun was up. The wheel of a cart, the blade of an axe. And they say, do not talk of these things.

(*Pause*)

STARLING: These clothes are coming out more dirty than they went in.
JACKER: I was robbed once, on my way back from the river. All my clean clothes gone.
STARLING: On your way back, that's bad. Best be robbed on your way there.
GRETA: What did you tell your husband?
JACKER: Tell? Nothing to *tell*. Went out arms full, came back arms empty. One look was enough, and then the back of his hand. (*Spits*) May he rot.
GRETA: He's dead?
JACKER: As dead as your grandfather's prick.
GRETA: Then whose clothes you washing?
JACKER: That was the first husband. Second went the same way. This 'uns the third. (*Throws the clothes down*) Three weeks, and I'm sick of the bastard. (*Picks up the spade, starts digging a hole*) See here earth, I know you're hungry. Here's his clothes for now. The man'll come later.

(*She shovels the clothes into the hole.*
YAXLEY *comes on in his underwear*)

YAXLEY: (*To* **JACKER**) Where's my trousers — they done yet?
AGNES: Where's your receipt?
YAXLEY: Receipt, what receipt. I don't need a receipt for my own property.
STARLING : No more property now, brother. You need a receipt.
YAXLEY: (*Indicates* **JACKER**) *She's* my receipt. (*To* **JACKER**) Where's them trousers?

JACKER: Ground's eaten 'em.
YAXLEY: Ground my arse.

(*He sees the trousers in the hole*)

You're looking for a thrashing.
GRETA: (*Advancing on* **YAXLEY**) Let's dump him in the river.
AGNES: Fool — we have to wash clothes in that.
JACKER: (*Advancing also*) No — let's kill him with the back of this spade. Bury him with his trousers.

(*The four women are moving towards* **YAXLEY**)

YAXLEY: (*Backing away*) Mad bitches.
    / What's got into you? (*Goes*)
AGNES: Come on, the earth's still hungry.

(*The women throw all the remaining clothes into the hole.*)

SCENE NINETEEN: THE SILVER PLATE

(*Camp. Late afternoon.*
WYAND *is standing beside a newly dug grave. Facing him,* **MOW** *and* **JIG**)

WYAND: From the day we are born, our grave is walking beside us. Like a hole in the world that is always waiting.
    / This could be your grave today. Or, you could be in heaven.
JIG: How we all going to fit in there, brother?
WYAND: Do all the sun's rays not fit on the earth? Do you believe that after death you shall still have this earthly body? Your earthly body is but a garment, a winter coat to throw away when summer comes.
MOW: I always keep mine.
WYAND: No — you shall be as a ray of light brother, and there will be room for you in heaven, even as there is room for the sun's rays on earth. (*Holding up one hand*) "For I say unto you who are suffering: God will give you rest. But when the Lord Jesus Christ appears suddenly from heaven in flaming fire with his mighty angels, bringing *vengeance* on them that do not know God — *then* shall they be punished with everlasting banishment from the presence of the Lord, and be cast into the firey pit".
MOW: I seen that. Where they burn the her ...
JIG: Heretics.
WYAND: But see how you may be saved: (*Holding up one hand*) "For we know if our earthly house of this tabernacle were dissolved, we have a building of God, an house not made with hands, eternal in the heavens".
    / Now. If you would live in that house, then follow me to the river, where I may wash away your sins in the name of the Lord.

JIG: Wash. Nobody said anything about that. I reckon I'll live in that house dirty, brother.

(**WYAND** *looks at* **MOW**)

MOW: That's what I say.
WYAND: But you shall not be let *in* dirty. Do you hear?

(*They stare at him*)

WYAND: (*Sudden change*) Well uck you then, uck and ugger you, you rastards. (*He goes out.*)

(**MOW** *takes out the silver plate from under his shirt, looks at his face in it.*)

JIG: What you going to do with it?
MOW: (*Dropping the plate into the grave*) Hide it in the grave, Agnes said. No one look in a grave.

(*He throws earth over it*)

JIG: Cept God. But I reckon he got enough plates already.

SCENE TWENTY : WATCHERS ON THE TOWER

(*Early evening. A watchtower near the camp.*
JACKER *and* **HOWLING** *are above, keeping watch.* **SEVERAL, SYMOND,** *and* **JIG** *are sitting below.*
SYMOND *is making a small model of a house, using mud*)

JACKER: (*To* **HOWLING**) Look at that cloud. Heaven is low today.
SEVERAL: (*From below*) All the better brother, to scoop up the souls of the dead.
JACKER: Who is that?
HOWLING: (*Looking down*) Several. And his boy. And the other one.
   / (*To* **JACKER**) What you looking at?
JACKER: The sky. Like a city in flames.

(*Pause*)

JIG: (*To* **SYMOND**) What you making?
SYMOND: Nothing.

(*He stares at the mud house, then gently knocks it down and starts again*)

HOWLING:(*After a pause*) My body's had enough of sweet, sticky days. The summer's worn out.
JACKER: I want the cold: the real thing. The heat's too gossipy, crawling everywhere. Cold's different: nails you in one place, like a spear.

(*Pause*)

HOWLING:You know how a day suddenly goes down for no reason? In the morning it smells fresh and there's a breeze blowing, blowing that freshness into your life. But come afternoon and it's all blown out; it's just sitting there, all sweet and heavy. But still clinging to you, like a woman you've grown tired of.

(*Pause*)

JACKER: Needs a storm. To break it.
HOWLING: (*Musing to himself*) Just a heavy old woman, that's all it is.
　　/ What are we guarding, can anyone tell us?
JACKER: (*Doesn't answer*)
SEVERAL: The sweat of thirty thousand armpits, Mow's silver plate, Agnes's bad temper …
SYMOND: Nothing.

(*He stares at the mud house, gently knocks it down and starts again*)

HOWLING: Always that echo.
　　/ What we need is a good rain.
JACKER: Always makes my bones ache. Why's that?
HOWLING: (*Doesn't answer*)
SEVERAL: It's because …
HOWLING: If you keep interrupting I shall come down and knock you into many pieces, and then you will be several indeed.

(*Pause/**SEVERAL** gets out his head on a stick and pretends to throttle it*)

JACKER: (*To* SEVERAL) Tell us then, wiseacres.

(*Far off, bleating is heard*)

But what is that, the bleating of lambs? I thought we had killed all the lambs.
HOWLING: Killed them all, yes, but then they sent for more.
JACKER: Who did, the city?
HOWLING: The butchers, yes. Killing is profit, even in wartime. What did you want to know? (*Musing to himself*) Is that what we are guarding, lambs?
JACKER: About the rain. (*To* SEVERAL) Tell us quickly, whilst the lambs are still bleating.

(*Pause/far off, the bleating continues*)

SEVERAL: Our bodies ache because we come from the sea. The rest of us has forgotten, but deep inside us the bones still remember. And cry out when they smell water.

(*Pause/the bleating dies away*)

JACKER: What is that to the south?
HOWLING: Looks like a swarm of bees.
/ Or a cloud ... of dust.

(**SYMOND** *has been staring at the mud house. He suddenly knocks it down, viciously this time, and then goes to make it again*)

SEVERAL: Stop.
/ What do you hope to build?
SYMOND: Nothing.
SEVERAL: (*Pointing to the heap of mud*) But you have already built it.
/ (*Perhaps showing himself for the first time*) Now do likewise in your heart.

(*He suddenly begins a violent drumming*)

AIE! AIE! AIE!

(**JIG** *begins a slow mock-solemn dance on his pipes, accompanied by* **SEVERAL's** *drumming.*
SYMOND *stares at the mud. Then he leaps up and kicks it, scattering it all over. He begins dancing, with a joyous intensity*)

HOWLING: (*Shouts down*) A CLOUD OF DUST. APPROACHING TO THE SOUTH.

(*The next passage should be shouted in an ever-increasing frenzy, accompanied by* **SEVERAL'S** *drumming*

SEVERAL: WHAT IS APPROACHING TO THE SOUTH?
JIG: (*Stops playing*) A CLOUD OF DUST!
SEVERAL: WHAT IS APPROACHING TO THE SOUTH?
SYMOND: A CLOUD OF DUST!
SEVERAL: A CLOUD OF DUST IS APPROACHING TO THE SOUTH!!
JIG: TO THE SOUTH IS APPROACHING A CLOUD OF DUST!!
SYMOND: TO THE SOUTH A CLOUD OF DUST IS APPROACHING!!
ALL THREE: TO THE SOUTH!!! A CLOUD OF DUST IS APPROACHING!!!
SYMOND: (*Stomping up and down on the mud*) AIE! AIE! AIE!

(*A few moments of total frenzy, whilst* **HOWLING** *and* **JACKER** *look on, amazed.*
Then: blackout/sudden silence, except for **SEVERAL's** *drumming, which continues for a few more seconds before fading away*)

SCENE TWENTY-ONE : THE LAST NIGHT

(**JIG's** *pipes are heard, playing a slow lament ('I heard a voice').*
The camp. Night.
Seated around a fire are **JIG, SEVERAL, SYMOND, GRETA, AGNES,**
YAXLEY, STARLING, HOWLING, *and* **JACKER. YAXLEY** *and*
HOWLING *are playing cards.*
Apart from the others, **YSOD.**
The pipes continue to play under the following lines)

JACKER: Can't see a thing for this smoke.
STARLING: What is there to see? It's *night*.
GRETA: (*To* **SYMOND**) What are you thinking of?
SYMOND: My grandfather's bald head. Everything else has vanished.
JACKER: (*To herself*) May as well fight. No point in going home. No one'll recog-
nise you.

(**HOWLING** *is staring at a card*)

STARLING: (*Leaning over to look*) The hanged man.
HOWLING: I want to look at him, stare him in the face.
YAXLEY: You'll do that tomorrow soon enough.
HOWLING: I would like to make my own death. In a battle, with thousands slain
all around you, how can you make your own death?

(*The sound of* **JIG's** *pipes fades away.*
THE HOODED MAN *enters and squats down outside the circle*)

SEVERAL: We do not need to make death, brother. He is already within us, from
the first day of our lives. A tiny thing, but growing on our own fear. Fat, on our
own fear. We eat, and he eats with us. We touch a lover's breast, and he is there at
the ends of our fingers. It is within us we must face him, not at the point of an
enemy's sword.
/ But if we starve him, he is but the banging of a door between one room
and the next.
STARLING: It is not only fear. There are many things in this life that I am not
weary of: the sun creeping over the leaves at dawn, my own face staring up at me
from the river, Mow's stupidity, Agnes's two eyes looming out of the dark like
moons ...
AGNES: (*Irritated*) And how long have you been seeing these things? All your life,
is it? Or just the last six weeks? Did you see them in the days of the black harvests,
when you were being driven from field to field like a crow, with no place to lay
your head?
(*Imitates* **STARLING**) "My stomach is empty, but oh the beauty of the leaves!"
(*Normal voice*) Did you ever say that? No. But now your stomach is full, you suddenly see them. (*Imitates*) "Oh, do not let me die, for the beauty of the leaves!"
(*Normal voice*) It is *that* which we fight for, can you not see?
STARLING: What.

AGNES: Full stomachs and the beauty of the leaves.

(*Laughter*)

Laugh, but would you go back to eating berries from the woods? Then go now, we have no use for you.

(*Pause*)

JACKER: It is true: our lives before were one long sleep.
HOWLING: When my hand froze to the bucket on a winter morning, was I then asleep? When the pitchfork went through my foot last harvest and I bled for three days, was that the blood of a dream?
JACKER: I did not mean ...
STARLING: But is it so precious, this new life, that we must die to hold on to it?
JIG: And what will it be to us then, when we are dead?
GRETA: But are all lives not precious, even the enemy's life?
THE HOODED MAN: It is life itself that is precious, not our own life.

(*Pause*)

YAXLEY: What is your hundred, brother?
THE HOODED MAN: The hundred of Wymondham[3] .
HOWLING: Kett's hundred.
THE HOODED MAN: Just so, brother.
YAXLEY: Come, warm yourself by the fire.
THE HOODED MAN: Thank you brother, but the night is warm enough.

(*Pause*)

SYMOND: (*To* **THE HOODED MAN**) Are we here then, just ... to live?
THE HOODED MAN: Not just to live, but to use up our lives. What a waste, if we do not do that. And think how it was before we came to this place: life used up *us*.

(*He moves, but not closer to them*)

Have we not lived for these six weeks in a great and joyous *freedom*, free at last to breathe under the sky and walk where we please on the earth? Without having to toil for an ungrateful master or wander the roads in search of shelter? When we are hungry we eat, when thirsty we drink. We have all we need here, and nothing we do not need. And have we not enjoyed true friendship, free of master and servant?
   / We have discovered how to live. And for that, they would kill us.
   / / But there is pain in this new freedom. And a wanting to go back, back to a time when we did not know this pain. For we were then living in a dungeon, and our pain was as the dark air of the dungeon, and we could not see it with our eyes

---

[3] Pronounced Wind-um (Author's note).

because our eyes knew nothing else. But now we have knocked down the dungeon, and our eyes are dazzled at this great light. Would you now close your eyes, and run back blind to the dungeon? But the dungeon is in ruins, and we are building here something far greater: *ourselves*.

(*Pause*)

SYMOND: (*Low, to* **GRETA**) It is him I told you of.
THE HOODED MAN: Think of us now as this: as grains of sand in one brick of a vast building. A building that will take many lifetimes to complete. But here we have already begun to build: a room. And he, the building, is aware of this — just as we are aware of the least tremor in our blood. And he needs us, this great building, to make himself complete — to feel that he *could* be complete. And if we have truly lived — even for a few seconds, before our death — then we have helped build him. For what we have done here, what we have *been* here, cannot be undone — not by flames, or racks, or armies. Because the room is already springing up, here in our hearts. And will survive us.

(*Pause*)

JACKER: But can we not still ... win?
STARLING: We are not here to win, but to lose — don't you know that yet?
JACKER: But do we have to die, so that other people will remember us?
YSOD: We are not here to die or to lose. Now is the time for fighting.

(*Pause*)

THE HOODED MAN: Just so.

(*Pause*)

SYMOND: (*Nervous but determined*) You speak of this thing we build up. And you seem to say: be the hero of your own life. And you give this thing no name, but you seem to say: God. And you say: be him, becoming him. And you seem to say: have pride in him, this becoming building.
/ But I say this: God does not dwell in what is built, but in what is taken away. Not in pride, or the memory of pride, but in its absence.

(*Pause*)

THE HOODED MAN: You are much in the way of 'seems', brother.
SYMOND: Not so brother, it is the seams are in the way of me. And I would cut these seams, and throw away the garment.

(*Pause*)

YAXLEY: What is the purpose of learning these things now, when we are this close to death?
STARLING:(*To herself*) All this about death.

THE HOODED MAN: (*To* **YAXLEY**) Long after our deaths, what we learn *now* will still be going about its business. And in that, we shall live. For this is our essence. And they will remember us in our essence, as one does a dead person.

(*Pause*)

GRETA: (*To* **SYMOND**) I shall be passed on as a smile at last, and you — for the way you hold that cup.
JIG: What is the earth made of, if not dead people. (*Takes out an apple*) There's only one thing to do with death, (*Bites into the apple*) and that's to eat it.
THE HOODED MAN: (*Stands*) Goodnight brothers.
SYMOND: (*Directly to him*) It should be of nothing, this building.
SEVERAL: (*Touching* **SYMOND's** *arm*) Peace, brother. It is of no account.

(**THE HOODED MAN** *looks hard at* **SYMOND** *before turning away to talk to* **YSOD**)

AGNES: What do we fight for? Nothing. A roof. Is this a roof? I come from a ditch. At night I slept under stars. For three years, since they pushed me off my land. Before that, the corner of a barn. Straw. Now what: leaves. Leaves in August. What shall there be in November, January? Stars again. Is that a roof, stars? If I leave here, what do I go back to? A ditch. Stars. Where is the roof?
     / And yet I shall fight.

(*Pause*)

HOWLING: He never said roof. *Room*, he said.
AGNES: Room.
THE HOODED MAN: (*Turning back to them*) As a great cathedral, but open to the sky.
STARLING: Hm. Open to the sky is bad. Could we not just ...
SYMOND: (*Cutting in, to* **STARLING**) Not open to the sky, *but in the very sky itself, open to everything* — do you not see? (*He looks at* **THE HOODED MAN**)
STARLING: It is *night*, fool — how can I see what is in the sky?

(**THE HOODED MAN** *stares back at* **SYMOND**, *then turns to go*)

YSOD: (*Privately*) Master.
THE HOODED MAN: I am no man's master, Ysod.
YSOD: (*Acknowledges this*)
     / That boy ...
THE HOODED MAN: Tomorrow, after the battle, if there is a he, an I, and a you — we shall speak of him. (*Goes*)

(**JIG** *begins playing his pipes quietly*)

SEVERAL: (*Sings*)
                    I heard a voice
                              from under a wall

the song it sang

          was old as earth:

"Until you take

          your hand from my throat

you'll never know

          what I am worth".

I heard a song

          as I walked out

under a dark

          and stormy sky:

"Until you take

          your hands from your face

you'll never see

          how others die".

(*Lights fade to black*)

SCENE TWENTY-TWO : BATTLE

(*Only* **AGNES'** *face is seen, bathed in a red light. All else is in darkness*)

AGNES: In the bright morning this thing came upon us like it was a many-sided monster, all gleaming and swarming with life. And in its eyes I saw our fear, reflected. There was flame, and smoke too, and it gathered volumes of us up and thrust us into its stomach. But there was scarce peace there, for all I could hear was the breaking of bones and the cries of my companions. And then, silence. And we became that silence: as smoke becomes air, or the drowned become the ocean.

(**AGNES'** *face disappears as the red light moves to the centre of the playing area. It remains there, a single spot, for a few seconds, then grows to envelop the audience. Simultaneously fade up the sound of a battle — human cries, horses, the clash of weapons — until it is deafening.*

Then cut sound/simultaneous blackout.)

SCENE TWENTY-THREE : CODA : NOTHING BUT NOTHING

[*Winter. Late afternoon.*

Same location as Scene Nineteen.

Wind, mud, dead leaves.

HUCK, CLOCK *and* **THE PRINCE OF MASTURBATORS** *are standing by the grave.* **THE PRINCE** *is now almost blind*)

HUCK: Is this the place?

CLOCK: She's lucky to have a grave, all the rest were burnt.
HUCK: This wind.
THE P OF M: (*Sharp*) Don't mention it.

    (**HUCK** *and* **CLOCK** *start digging*)

HUCK: At least there's no more smoke. The smoke, eh Prince, when they were burning the bodies from the battle? And the flames as tall as buildings, flaring up into the night.
CLOCK: The stink of it.

    (*Pause/digging continues*)

THE P OF M: The air is cold and yet I can see leaves on that tree. Fat young leaves, swaying about in the ... (*Clears his throat*)
CLOCK: (*Stops digging, looks*) Birds. (*Quietly*) They're birds, Prince.
THE P OF M: Birds? (*Looks again*)

    (*Pause/digging continues*)

HUCK: (*Stops*) See how the leaves are changing to mud.
CLOCK: We're starving to death and you talk of leaves?
THE P OF M: (*Quietly*) Everything's mud in the end.
HUCK: And the sun, throwing shadows on the hill's rim.
CLOCK: (*Stops digging*) Leaves, is it? (*Grabs* **HUCK** *by the throat*) We're starving to death! We're starving to death!
HUCK: (*Struggling*) Clock is starving to death, go down sun! Don't change, leaves!

    (*Pause/they glare at each other*)

THE P OF M: (*Suddenly*) It is when we are alive we should flare up, not when we are dead.
CLOCK: (*Goes up to him*) Why this sadness, Prince?
THE P OF M: My eyes. (*He takes a woman's shoe from his pocket and holds it up to his face*) I can't see to steal.
CLOCK: My eyes get bigger as the rest of me gets smaller. (*Looks down*) They'll soon be all that's left of me.
HUCK: (*Starts digging again*) You'll be able to fit in anywhere, like the wind.
THE P OF M: (*Sharp*) *I said not to mention the wind.*

    (*Pause/* **HUCK** *digs up the silver plate.*
    CLOCK *and* **THE PRINCE OF MASTURBATORS** *turn to look*)

HUCK: (*Holding the plate up to her face*) "It must be mine, it's got my face on it".
    / We'll get drunk tonight, Prince.
THE P OF M: And then what. Nothing.

    / Nothing and nothing but.
CLOCK: What?

THE P OF M: When we worked in the fields we had pain and nothing but. And when we took to the roads we had cold and nothing but. For six weeks in the Great Camp we had excitement and nothing but. And then before the battle we had fear and nothing but; and we ran, and those who stayed were killed and burnt. And for six days we had smoke and nothing but. And then the wind came, and blew away the smoke. And now we have nothing. Nothing but nothing.

> (*They freeze.*
> *Lights fade down/sound of wind increases slightly.*
> **AGNES, GRETA, SEVERAL, JIG, SYMOND, YSOD, YALLOP, STARLING** *and* **WILSE** *enter silently and stand in a circle around the edge of the playing area. Their faces, hair, and clothes are streaked with blood.*
> **HUCK, CLOCK** *and* **THE PRINCE OF MASTURBATORS** *remain frozen and appear not to notice them.*)

AGNES: Even the earth, this huge magnet,
cannot hold us.
We rise as smoke,
as the memory of smoke.

/ Most live as wood,
to be cut down and fashioned,
each to his own particular shape:
some serve, as a table;
some wage war, as a club;
most stay shut, as a door.
(Each thing holding within it
the fear of flames).

/ But we are smoke.
Suddenly, we were smoke.
To use up your life,
that is the hardest thing.

> (*As lights fade down to black, fade up the sound of wind.*)

APPENDIX: SCENE THIRTEEN (ALTERNATIVE VERSION)

This scene may need to be adapted to suit the theatre space in which the play is being performed. At Manchester Royal Exchange, for example, sticks left behind from Scene Twelve were used to represent the gradual growth of the I. The scene was played as follows:

SYMOND: (*Restless*) Why is everything so difficult?
WILSE: What is? The sky does not find things difficult, neither does the earth.
SYMOND: I am not the sky or the earth.
WILSE: Oh — I, is it? but does this I not touch them? Look.

(*She picks up a long stick and breaks two small pieces off it, then lays the three pieces on the ground in the shape of an I*)

I

Here is your I. Long and narrow, with a roof for the sky and two feet for the earth. See how thin it is, this I of yours — almost invisible. And yet joined to everything. But now see what happens. The I is not satisfied with earth and sky, it has to grow fat of itself, look — see how your name adds to its volume.

(*She picks up another stick and uses it to scratch his name in the dirt, speaking it aloud as she does so*)

SYMOND

And as you grow older, the I grows more and more. You were a ... shoe-maker.

(*She adds another stick, partially obscuring the name:*)

SYIMOND

And then an … actor.

(*She adds another stick:*)

What next. Perhaps a … soldier.

(*She adds another stick*)

SIIIMOND

Or even a … lover.

(*She adds another stick*)

SII II I OND

See how the poor I is pulled this way and that. So important, so heavy - and yet the true I is lost. Now.

(*She picks up the sticks and scrubs out the name, then puts down more sticks, this time in a different arrangement*)

You and your brothers. What do they most resemble?

> (**SYMOND** *puzzles over it.* **WILSE** *adds some white rags and scratches the shape of the sun on the ground*)

SYMOND: The rain, that falls between sky and earth.
WILSE: Just so. (*Putting down more sticks, naming each one as she does so*) Symond. Greta. Ysod. Jig. And each drop unique, a clear crystal. But look.

> (*She throws down a stick on top of the drawing*)

Shoemaker.

> (*Throws down another stick*)

Actor.

> (*Throws down another stick*)

Soldier.

> (*Throws down another stick*)

Lover.
SYMOND: (*Throwing down a stick*) Girl.
WILSE: (*Throwing down a stick*) Mother.
SYMOND: (*Throwing down a stick*) Thief.
WILSE: (*Throwing down a stick*) Spy.
SYMOND: (*Throwing down a stick*) Beggar.
WILSE: (*Throwing down a stick*) Dreamer.
SYMOND: (*Throwing down a stick*) Leader.
WILSE: (*Throwing down a stick*) Rebel.
SYMOND: (*Throwing down a stick*) Brother!

(The drawing should now look something like)

WILSE: The I's are lost and scream for attention. Even in the brightest day, there is a great darkness because of the jumble of I's

(**SYMOND** *walks away, thinking*)

SYMOND: (*Turns and comes back*) But is there not a great comfort in this darkness, a comfort in knowing that the I is not alone, and all others are similarly dark?
WILSE: It is true, there is a great and false comfort.
SYMOND: But the true I, the I that lives in the light, is this not be terribly alone?

(*Pause*)

WILSE: Think of the rain, brother: I's like rods of water. Like rods of rain falling.

Contemporary Theatre Review,
1996, Vol. 5, 3–4 pp. 87–94
Reprints available directly from the publisher
Photocopying permitted by license only

ROD WOODEN'S *SMOKE* : TOO EARLY OR TOO LATE?

Meral Taygun

"Why can't this earth, even this huge magnet hold us", that,
"We rise as smoke, as the memory of smoke"?
Why are we so comfortably numbed by this scientific age of ours, which hands out pre-determined "fast" answers to hypothetical questions?
Why are we so resilient to statements as; "History simply repeats itself"?
Why are we in such a hurry that we are getting less and less eager to listen; to hear in order to re-hear and communicate?
Why are we so scared to be confronted with "the memory of **SMOKE**"?

Too Early or Too Late?

Today, in a world of production and management, words like: aggression, execution, ambition, opportunity, stupidity and contact, are exchanging mantles with: passion, performance, dreams, ideals, innocence and friendship.

Words are getting catalogued and categorized under : 'eras' and political views. They are being fingered through, accepted or rejected according to the fashion of the day. And Thesaurus is pretty unfashionable nowadays.

Our languages are being stripped of their sentiments and images. Our words are becoming mere symbols in getting us through a life, geared towards commerce. We are dreaming of winning and power; having nightmares of losing control and failing. To fit a pre-designed graphics of "life achievement" is getting to be our main goal in life.

We have either sold out our stories, or lost touch with them behind self-built walls of protection; alienating ourselves from ourselves, and from the others. Our fear of being vulnerable is growing in direct ratio to our paranoia. Consciously or unconsciously we are divorcing our worlds from the worlds of those who still dare to be vulnerable enough to hang on to their stories, to listen to others; and are reaching out to communicate. We are aborting our own languages to adopt the brutal, freak off-spring of the media.

We are transforming into insensitive robots in flesh and blood.

Several years ago Ms Cicely Berry said "Our eyes have eaten away our ears". Is that all that our eyes have eaten away?

Our eyes have eaten away our minds; our hearts. They have even eaten away themselves. We are beginning to think, feel and see through the spectacles handed down to us by the remote-control buttons of the TV screens; and the news media.

We look to stare; we hear to judge.

We throttle our basic instincts to love and be loved; to care and be eased for; to create and to preserve. A sado-masochistic, elitist drive – to be bigger than life –

makes us take refuge in the false comfort of the arrogant fashionable attitude of "the modern times": cynical nihilism.

Rod Wooden's *Smoke* was written and staged 48 years after World War II; which ended with the motto:

"We will never forget. We shall never let it happen again"

Did we forget? We seem to be letting it happen again.

Smoke appears on the stage when the world is busy tearing down concrete walls only to replace them with thicker invisible ones. More and more nations are dividing into even more nations, under more new national flags. Every separated unit is creating "the other" while re-creating itself. Every suppressed dream, hatred and anger is surfacing, blaming "the other" and giving birth to new animosities, new defences and new crimes.

The Barbarians never arrived in Cavafy's *The Barbarians are Coming*. How could we arrive when we are already there.

Smoke is self-confronting and, probably, self-confrontation is one of the most difficult things, when we all seem to be hanging on to the bobbing neck of some fake horse, on this guilt-ridden, opinionated merry-go-round.

Smoke is not a comfortable play with a natural flow and a naturalistic structure. It is an epic argumentation piece. It is a testimony in fragments. It evokes feeling but not empathy; it stirs up thoughts without intellectuality. It leaves us free to disagree. There are no easy heroes, no obvious villains. Any identification that occurs with a figure gets broken by the same figure at another instant, in another situation. The characters are changeable and realistic. Nevertheless, behind all this realism there is an amazing poetic musicality. *Smoke* is a rare example of poetic realism.

'Norfolk 1549. A time of bitterness, great riches, and hunger.' ... A group of banished, rejected, exiled outcasts resolve to survive together with their differences under the protection of the word: Brotherhood. Or do they?

Their hopes and wishes, their fears and mistakes, are turned into fables and songs by an actor, and get re-presented back to them for their entertainment.

Smoke takes us through the brief life of this community which only lasts for six months before it meets its' evitable or inevitable end. The play re-states problems, the solution of which are not yet found. It starts a journey not completed. It is an unfinished symphony. That's where the hope lies: there is always a "yet" to come.

Smoke is like an important but tiny article crushed between ads at the bottom of the tenth page of a newspaper. It may escape our attention, deeply attract it; or it may be one we choose to ignore.

It is Breugel's, *The Fall of Icarus*: ... a society so busy with other things, that it completely misses a young man's invincible attempts to fly.

But today we do fly.

Smoke is like a series of ballads of cultures, races, genders, and of their convictions, dreams and beliefs. This is the universal quality of *Smoke*. I can imagine the play in any language, on any stage of the world. Perhaps more so than in the Western languages and for the Western public. It is a call on ears open to receive this 'epique pastorale' with their inner ears.

But somehow the whole story, style, music, characters and the vision within and beyond the *Smoke* is too demanding on the impatient, success oriented, CNN conditioned, Coca-Cola edited, commercially-brainwashed Western mentalities of ours. We tend to react too hastily to "les voix humaines" with our usual arrogant, euro-centric, tongue-in-cheek prejudiced attitudes.

We'd rather push the next button. Find the next channel. Turn it off. Take the next corner; not look back. "Discover" the "new" .. Catch the next flight .. move on to the next opportunity. Get away from it all. Get away from the *Smoke*, from "the memory of Smoke"...

If we can.

On Directing *Smoke*, in Holland

Directing *Smoke* in Dutch has been one of the most pleasant periods of my life. The whole process had started on a positive note to begin with. The play, which I was to have been a part of in Manchester,[1] was read by students of mine who were dedicated to establishing the peace in Sarajevo; who begged me to ask Mr Wooden if he would let them perform it, to be dedicated to their cause, under my direction.

My first instinct was only to do a reading of the play, if we could get Mr Wooden's consent; and if we had a good translation.

Mr Wooden generously gave his consent. This was March 1994. We had a deadline. The show or the reading had to be out by the first week of June. Ronald Ockhuysen – one of the theatre critics of the Dutch daily *The Volkskrant* – having read and loved the play volunteered to translate it for us.

We spent the whole month of April reading only the English text; analysing it and breaking it down. Our translator was attending most of the meetings and bringing in translated material periodically. We were constantly going from one text to the other. All of the actors were fluent in English. This was making everything much more easy and fruitful. In the end, with Mr Ronald Ockhuysen's super-natural efforts and the dedication of the student actors, we had an excellent translation.

The quality of the translation started tempting me to actually stage the whole play, but something in me was not letting go of doing simply a reading.

We started rehearsing with the Dutch text in May. Within a week the young actors had memorised their lines, but for me they were still the story-tellers. With the arrival of the music it was getting impossible to keep them in their seats. Slowly they started sneaking in bits of costumes and props. And suddenly one day I arrived at the rehearsal to find a mountain: a mountain built out of dismountable class-room platforms, covered from the floor to the top out of a sheep-skin patchwork blanket which they had sewn over-night.

We decided to perform the play. But the show was not going to be bigger than the text. The actors were still going to be the story-tellers, the link between the public and the play.

My direction could be boiled down to:

> Don't perform. Be. Tell. Enjoy telling.

---

[1] Meral Taygun was unable to take part in the Manchester production because of problems with Equity which were related to the fact that she still carries a Turkish passport. (ed.)

We tried to build the characters, along with the story and the mountain, in front of the audience; till everything literally collapsed during the battle scene again in front of the audience. Agnes comes to finish the play only to re-start the story.

The arrival of Mr Wooden during the last days of the rehearsals was an enormous stimulus for the young actors. The work didn't stop. We were constantly changing things around, discussing, re-rehearsing scenes.

The opening night was not dreaded. The work had not stopped for us. We would talk to the members of the public, to colleagues and friends: we would get together among ourselves, call for rehearsals and put our work to a new test the next day.

The last performance was still like the first show for us all. We had just begun, tomorrow we would pay more attention to this or that.

Even though I believe we had the right approach to presenting *Smoke*, I still believe it needed more and more simplicity. Even though I think that we were on the right track to contacting the public, we still had moments of "acting", or "directing" in the show. And even though we tried to do justice to *Smoke*; I wonder if we really were as innocent and selfless to do so.

We had the pleasure of reaching the very young, the young, and the old. Sadly it was the generation in between who shut their doors to "the memory of Smoke" ....

October 1994
Meral Taygun
Artistic Director
Acting School of Amsterdam

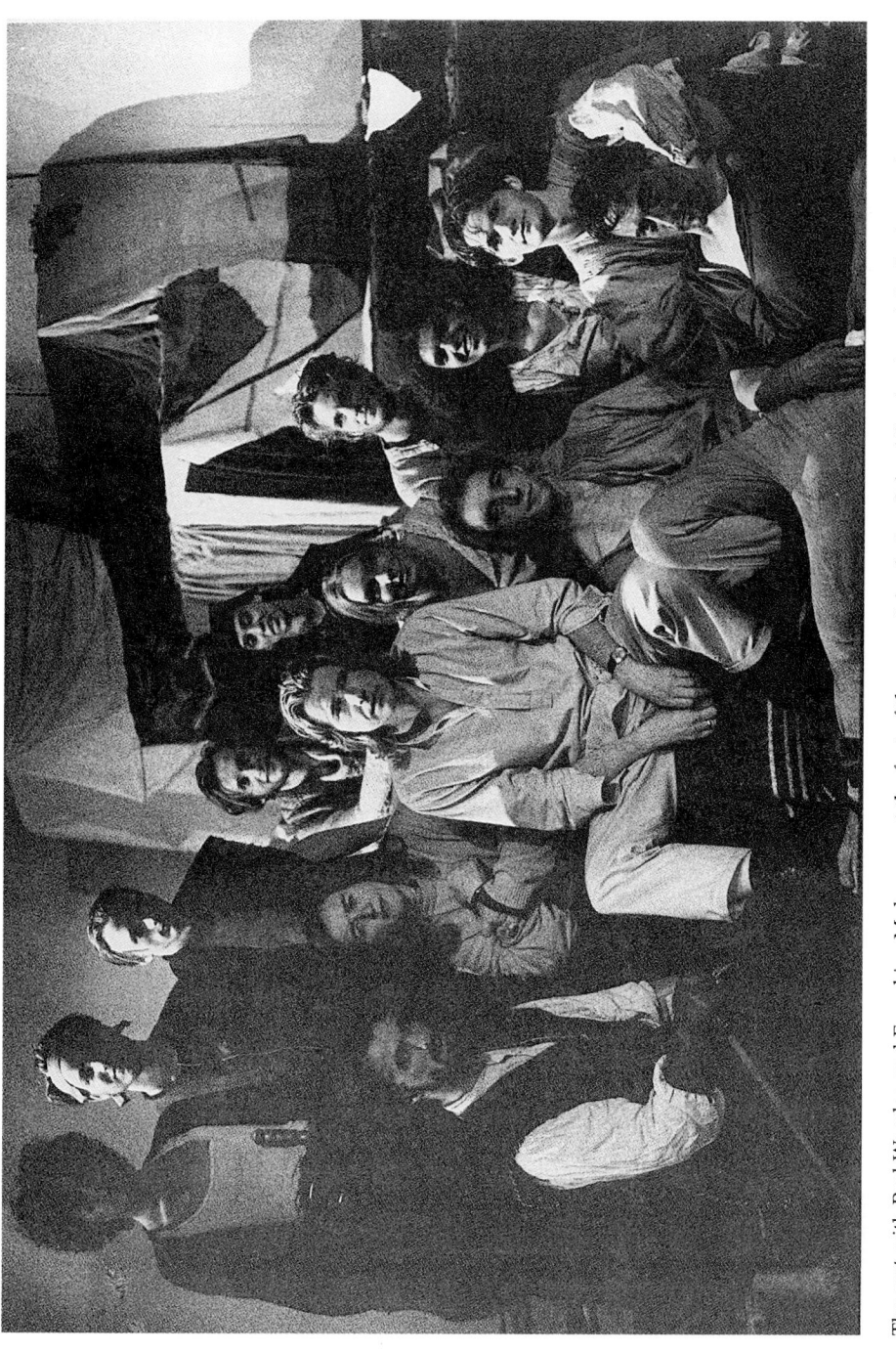

The cast with Rod Wooden and Franchine Mulrooney at the foot of the mountain. Acting School Production of *Smoke*, Amsterdam, June 1994.
Photo: Meral Taygun.

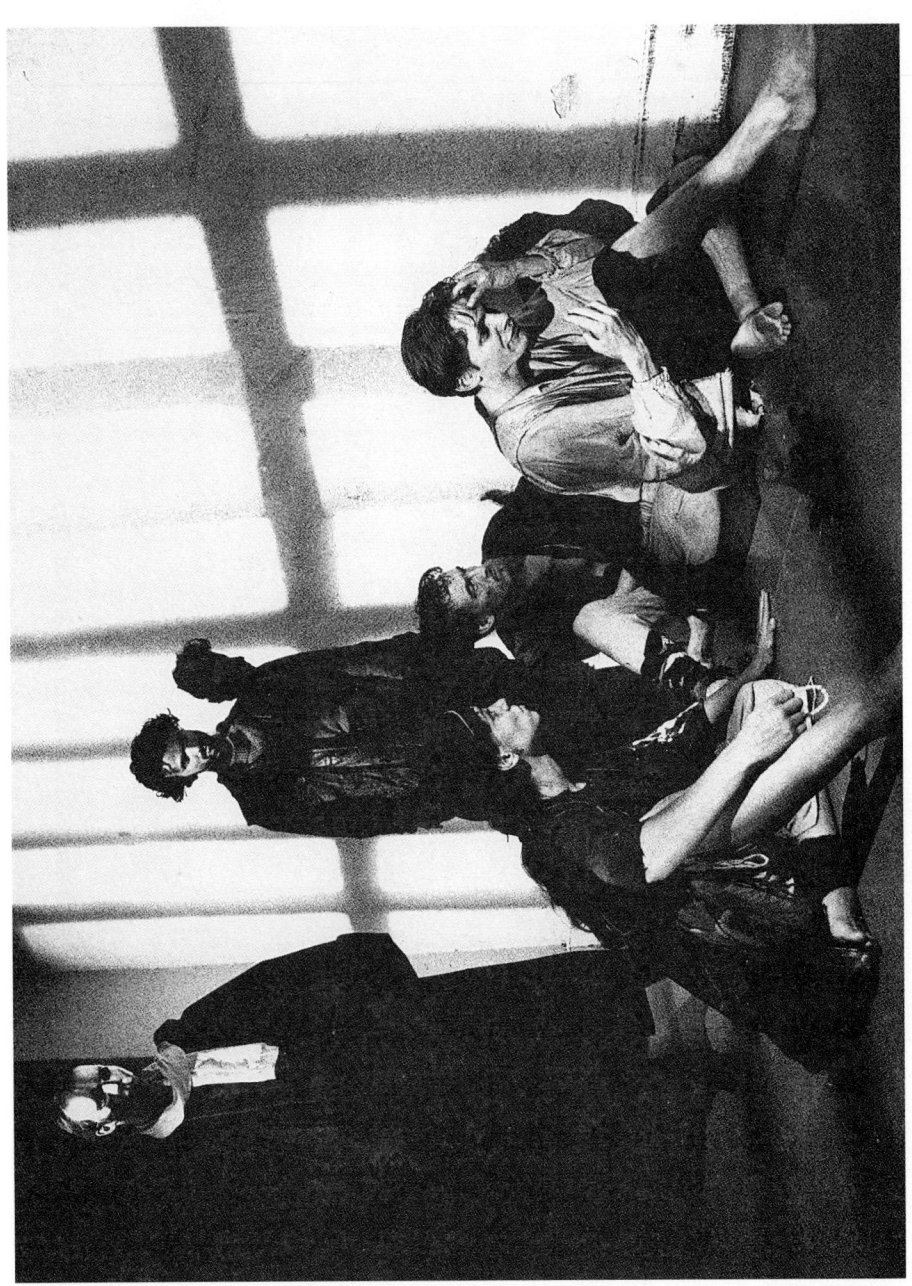

A piece of the night. Acting School Production of *Smoke*, Amsterdam, June 1994. Photo: Meral Taygun.

Watcher on the tower. Acting School Production of *Smoke*, Amsterdam, June 1994. Photo: Meral Taygun.

The clothers' river and the earth. Acting School Production of *Smoke*, Amsterdam, June 1994. Photo: Meral Taygun.

MOBY DICK

from the novel by Herman Melville

in a new version

by

Rod Wooden

Every angel is terrifying.
Rainer Maria Rilke: *The Duino Elegies*.

What it amounts to is that we are constantly permitting unpermissable things.
There are only a very few really permissable things: like the sea, for example.
Yukio Mishima: *The sailor who fell from grace with the sea*.

Contemporary Theatre Review,
1996, Vol. 5, 3–4 pp. 97–151
Reprints available directly from the publisher
Photocopying permitted by license only

LIST OF CHARACTERS

Aboard the ship 'Pequod':
CAPTAIN AHAB
STARBUCK, First Mate
STUBB, Second Mate
ISHMAEL
QUEEQUEG
PIP
DUNDEE
MANXMAN
TAHITI

Elsewhere:
MELVILLE
ELIJAH
CAPTAIN MAYHEW of the 'Jeroboam'
JEROBOAM'S OARSMAN
GABRIEL
CAPTAIN BOOMER of the 'Samuel Enderby'
JACK BUNGER, surgeon of the 'Samuel Enderby'
CAPTAIN GARDINER of the 'Rachel'

The play has been written for a company of nine male actors. The first four parts should not be doubled, except that ISHMAEL will also play MELVILLE. The other five actors (QUEEQUEG, PIP, DUNDEE, MANXMAN, and TAHITI) will play all the remaining parts.

GENERAL NOTES

THE SET should be kept as simple as possible. There are two basic locations: the ship's deck, and the sea. The deck should have three masts, one of which must be climbable; the other two masts may be represented by the mastheads only. All three mastheads should be combustible. The only other essentials are the tiller and some railing to represent the side of the ship. To one side of the deck is AHAB's cabin; in it, a table and chair, both screwed to the floor.

COSTUMES: the officers and CREW of the 'Pequod', plus ELIJAH, GABRIEL, and JEROBOAM'S OARSMAN should be rough and raggedy-looking, preferably unshaven. The visiting captains should be much neater, with the hint of a uniform. AHAB has a false leg (made of white whalebone) and a facial scar. TAHITI dresses entirely in black, AHAB sometimes wears a black slouch hat. THE WHALE should be the only thing in the play which is white in colour, except for the bedsheets and AHAB's false leg.

IN THE TEXT, the word CREW refers to everyone aboard the 'Pequod' except AHAB, STARBUCK, and STUBB; SHIP'S COMPANY refers to everyone except AHAB. The HELMSMAN and LOOK-OUT can be any member of THE CREW, and may be varied.

THE CHORUS: some of the choruses may be spoken by THE CREW as one unit, whilst others may be split between individual voices. An examples of how a chorus may be split between different voices is given in the fifth chorus of Scene Three.

INTERMISSION: if required, an intermission may be taken after Scene Twelve.

SONGS: 'In Christ there is no east or west' (Scene One) is an American hymn, written by John Oxenham and J.H.Fillmore (copyright Fillmore Bros. 1923).
   'The Whaling Song' (Scene One) is taken from 'Mocha Dick: the White Whale of the Pacific', an article by J.N.Reynolds which appeared in The Knickerbocker (New York Monthly Magazine XIII) of May 1839, and which was one of Melville's principal sources for 'Moby Dick'.
   'I don't want no long tall captain' and 'Early in the morning' (both Scene Eight) are based on American work songs; the words are mine, adapted from the originals.
   'Out on the waves' (Scenes Twelve and Seventeen) is based on the nineteenth century Irish 'Famine Song'; the words are mine, adapted from the original.

ACKNOWLEDGEMENT: in PIP's speech at the end of Scene Seven I have stolen a line from my own version of Buchner's *Woyzeck* — which in turn is adapted from a cancelled line in Buchner's original manuscript.

Rod Wooden
October 1993

This new version of **Moby Dick** was first performed by the Royal Shakespeare Company at The Other Place, Stratford Upon Avon on 20th October 1993, with the following cast:

Aboard the ship 'Pequod' :

CAPTAIN AHAB	David Calder
STARBUCK, FIRST MATE	Christopher Hunter
STUBB, SECOND MATE	Ray Fearon
ISHMAEL	David Birrell
QUEEQUEG	Christopher Colquhoun
PIP	Lloyd Notice
DUNDEE	Peter Grimes
MANXMAN	Simon Coury
TAHITI	Daniel York

Elsewhere :

MELVILLE	David Birrell
ELIJAH	Daniel York
CAPTAIN MAYHEW OF THE *JEROBOAM*	Daniel York
GABRIEL	Christopher Colquhoun
CAPTAIN BOOMER OF THE *SAMUEL ENDERBY*	Simon Coury
JACK BUNGER, SURGEON OF THE *SAMUEL ENDERBY*	Daniel York
CAPTAIN GARDINER OF THE *RACHEL*	Peter Grimes

Other parts played by members of the company.

Directed by Gerry Mulgrew
Designed by Karen Tennent
Composer and Musical Associate: Karen Wimhurst

Lighting designed by Robert Jones
Dialect Consultant: William Richards
Sound by Charles Horne
Company voice work by Andrew Wade and Cicely Berry

Stage Manager: Alison Owen
Deputy Stage Manager: Sue Gilligan
Assistant Stage Manager: Lynda Snowden

Musicans:
Trombone Kevin Pitt
Percussion James Jones

NB In the text that follows square brackets [ ] denote passages which were cut in the RSC production.

ONE : GOING ABOARD

(*A dark room.* **MELVILLE** *is sitting at a table, writing a letter. He wears outdoor clothes, muddy boots. To one side is a double bed with clean white sheets, the covers turned back.*)

MELVILLE: "I have a sort of sea-feeling here in the country, now that the ground is all covered with snow. I look out of my window in the morning when I rise as I would out of a porthole of a ship in the Atlantic. My own room seems a ship's cabin; and at nights when I wake up and hear the wind shrieking, I almost fancy there is too much sail on the house, and I had better go on the roof and rig in the chimney".

(*He throws down his pen, comes forward.*)

Domesticity — (*He glances behind him*) — it holds you fast, like an anchor. And yet — what is it? To feel a damp, drizzly November in your soul, and to do nothing about it except worry about clean sheets and hang about writing desks — when you should be stepping out into the street and methodically knocking people's hats off — is this not domesticity? And to write down that this is how I met him, and then him, and afterwards this, is that not domesticity also? And does this domesticity not nail you in one place, as the whale is nailed by the flying harpoon?

(*He goes to the bed and begins walking over the sheets in his muddy boots.*)

A plague on domesticity! Let this be of the flying harpoon, of the sea itself, or the very air.

(*He gets down from the bed.* **QUEEQUEG** *enters behind him, a harpoon in his hand.* **MELVILLE** *does not notice him.*)

Your true man should be as a savage, owing no allegiance but to the King of the Cannibals — and ready at any moment to rebel against him. I myself —

(**QUEEQUEG** *taps him on the shoulder with the harpoon.* **MELVILLE** *lets out a shriek.*)

QUEEQUEG: Dom — es — tissity. He must be a god, this dom — es — tissity, that you hate him so much.

(*Pause*)

You go whaling — (*points*) — on that ship?

(*Lights up on* **STARBUCK** *and* **STUBB** *standing by the mast.*)

STARBUCK: Ishmael — is that what you call yourself?

MELVILLE: (*Still with his back to them*) A plague on domesticity. This is other. (*He turns*) Yes, sir.
STARBUCK: Sign here then, Ishmael.

(**ISHMAEL** *does so, using the table.*)

ISHMAEL: Sir, I have a friend —
STUBB: Friend? What sort of friend? A hammock friend? A friend for three years and thrice around the world? A friend for the mingling of blood? A friend as I might say to you — look, *friend* ...? What kind of friend d'ye mean?
ISHMAEL: I mean — a kind of harpooner, sir. His name is Queequeg.
STUBB: Well now. (*Looking across*) Hey there, Quohog, did ye ever stand in the head of a whale-boat? Did ye ever strike a fish?
QUEEQUEG: See that drop of tar on the water, Captain? Well suppose that drop of tar is the whale's eye —

(*He throws the harpoon. It disappears into the black.*)

That whale's pretty much dead now, Captain.
STUBB: You better sign here, Quohog — know how to sign your name, do you? Or maybe you can just make a mark like this, eh ... (**QUEEQUEG** *is writing his name,* **STUBB** *looks over his shoulder*) ... Queequeg.

QUEEQUEG: I been ten years in this country, Captain. No talkee likee thisee any more.

(*Pause*)

STARBUCK: Captain Ahab is the captain of this ship.

(*Pause*)

But he's below, getting over a little sickness. You'll meet him soon enough. I am Starbuck, First Mate. And this is Mr. Stubb, Second Mate. Now, get your gear aboard — we sail with the tide. (*He turns away*) Hey you, Pip — and you, Manxman — stow these below.

(**PIP** *and* **MANXMAN** *come forward, remove the table and chair.*
ISHMAEL *and* **QUEEQUEG** *are walking off.*)

ISHMAEL: (*imitating* **STUBB**) Friend? What sort of friend?
QUEEQUEG: (*likewise*) A hammock friend?
ISHMAEL: (*more serious*) A friend for three years and thrice around the world?
QUEEQUEG: (*more serious still*): A friend for...(*holding out his hand*)...the mingling of blood?
(*A pause.* **ISHMAEL** *goes to take it. Before he can do so, an* **OLDER MAN** *who has been sitting at the side suddenly speaks to them.*)

THE MAN: Say men, have ye signed on that ship?

(*They stop*)

ISHMAEL: If you mean the Pequod, yes, we —
THE MAN: Anything down there about your souls?
QUEEQUEG: What?
THE MAN: Oh, perhaps you haven't got any. No matter, though — I know many as hasn't, and all the better for it they are too. A soul's a sort of fifth wheel to a wagon. Seen Old Thunder yet, have ye?
QUEEQUEG: Who?
THE MAN: Captain Ahab. Haven't seen him yet, have ye?
ISHMAEL: No — he's sick, they say. But he's getting better, and will be all right before long.
THE MAN: All right before long! When Captain Ahab is all right, this left arm of mine (*He holds up his left sleeve, it is empty*) will be all right, and not before. Still, someone's got to sail with him I suppose, and as well you as any others. (*He gets up, catching hold of* **ISHMAEL** *as he does so*) Going aboard then, are you?
ISHMAEL: Take your hands off, will ye? We're off to the Indian and Pacific Oceans, and would prefer not to be detained.
THE MAN: Oh you are, are ye? Coming back afore breakfast? (*Laughs, turns to go*) Morning to ye, shipmates, morning.
ISHMAEL: Morning it is. Come on, Queequeg. (*To* **THE MAN**) But wait, what's your name?

(**THE MAN** *is going off*)

Tell us your name, will you?
THE MAN: Elijah. And yours, shipmate?
ISHMAEL: (*To himself*) Call me Ishmael. (*Turns*) Call me —

(*But* **ELIJAH** *has gone*)

STUBB: (*Shouting across*) Are you men coming aboard, or not?

(**QUEEQUEG** *goes aboard,* **ISHMAEL** *follows. The whole* **SHIP'S COMPANY** *is now on deck*)

STUBB: Cast off there, Dundee! Lend him a hand, Tahiti!

(**ISHMAEL** *is standing near the gangplank, looking over the side.*)

ISHMAEL: This story of yours. Has it begun? How will it end? What shall be the middle of it? (*He puts his foot on the gangplank*)
DUNDEE: Avast! (*He pulls* **ISHMAEL** *on deck, then picks up the gangplank*)

(*The ship is now moving out to sea*)

DUNDEE: (*Shouting overboard*) Ahoy there! This is the Pequod, bound round the world! Tell them to address all future letters to the Pacific Ocean! And this time three years, if we are not back home, then address them to —

(*A wave crashes, drowning his words*)

STARBUCK: A hymn, men — a hymn for the voyage.

(*He begins to sing. The* **SHIP'S COMPANY** *come together and join in*)

STARBUCK
AND SHIP'S
COMPANY:

In Christ there is no east or west,
In Him no south or north;
But one great fellowship of love
Throughout the whole wide earth.
In Him shall true hearts everywhere
Their high communion find;
His service is the golden chord
Close binding all mankind.

Join hands then, brothers of the faith,
What e'er your race may be,
Who serves my father as a son
Is surely kin to me.
In Christ now meet both east and west,
In Him meet south and north;
All Christly souls are one in Him
Throughout the whole wide earth.

(*As the last note is held,* **STUBB** *breaks into a rollicking whaling song, which* **THE CREW** *take up as they return to their work*)

STUBB AND
CREW:

Don't bother my head about catching of seals
To me there's more glory in catching of eels
Just give me a tight ship, and under snug sail
And I ask for no more, alongside the sperm whale
        In the Indian Ocean
        Or Pacific Ocean
        No matter what ocean
        Pull ahead, yo heave O!

[Our boat's in the water, each man at his oar
Bends strong to the sea, while his bark bounds before
As the fish of all sizes, still flouncing and blowing
With fluke and broad fin, scorn the best of hard rowing
        Oh hang to the oar, boys
        Another stroke more, boys
        Now line up the oar, boys
        Pull ahead, yo heave O!

So give me a whaleman, wherever he be
Who fears not a fish that can swim the salt sea
Then give me a tight ship, and under snug sail

At last lay me 'side of the noble sperm whale
In the Indian Ocean
Or Pacific Ocean
No matter what ocean
Pull ahead, yo heave O!]

STUBB: (*As the song dies away*) Up helm! And keep her off around the world!

(*The sea crashes*)

TWO : A MOODY GOOD CAPTAIN

(**THE CREW** *are working on deck.* **ISHMAEL** *and* **QUEEQUEG** *are slightly apart from the others*)

DUNDEE: Funny how you never get wasps on a ship. Ever noticed that, have ye?
QUEEQUEG: (*To* **ISHMAEL**) Wasps?

(*Pause*)

ISHMAEL: (*To the others, attempting to start up a conversation*) What's he like, this Captain?
DUNDEE: No one's seen him.
ISHMAEL: No one?
DUNDEE: Not since the start of the voyage.
MANXMAN: Heard him, though.
QUEEQUEG: Heard him?
TAHITI: (*To himself*) Questions.
PIP: His white boot and his whalebone leg. (*Demonstrates*) On the deck. See?
ISHMAEL: Not exactly. What...
PIP: (*Eagerly*) They say he's got the sort of mouth would swallow an ocean, like Dundee (*Laughter from* **THE CREW**). Other times (*Going over to* **TAHITI**) he don't say nothing at all, he just looks at you. And he's moody, desperate moody sometimes, almost as moody as this old Manxman here. (*More laughter*)
ISHMAEL: Has anyone seen him laugh?
PIP: Laugh?

(*Pause*)

MANXMAN: Laugh. It's better to sail under a moody good captain, young feller, than a laughing bad one. Now this Ahab...

(**DUNDEE** *has been brooding to himself*)

DUNDEE: (*Suddenly, to* **PIP**) Don't call me bigmouth, boy.
PIP: Didn't.
DUNDEE: You calling me a liar, boy?

(*He springs at* **PIP** *and chases him around the deck. As they come round a second time,* **QUEEQUEG** *steps in front of* **DUNDEE** *and blocks his path.* **ALL** *freeze. There is a sudden clap of thunder*)

STUBB: (*Off*) Hands by the halyard! Stand by to reef topsails!

(**THE CREW** *scatter to their various tasks - except* **PIP**, *who cautiously creeps away*)

THREE : THE WHITENESS OF THE WHALE

(*Day.*
TAHITI, MANXMAN, *and* **PIP** *are working on deck, supervised by* **STUBB**. **AHAB** *enters and walks slowly around the deck; he is immersed in his own thoughts, looks at no one.* **THE CREW** *continue their work, but glance nervously at him from time to time.*
   AHAB *stops for a moment, then starts off again — at which point* **STUBB** *approaches him*)

STUBB: Captain Ahab, sir —

(**AHAB** *turns and looks at him*)

You disturb the men's sleep, sir.

(*Pause /* **AHAB** *continues to look at him*)

The night watch, sleeping below — you disturb their sleep, sir, with your leg.

(*Pause /* **THE CREW** *have stopped work*)

AHAB: Sleep. (*Then, suddenly*) What is sleep if it is not dreaming of whales? What is being awake if it is not showing a readiness for whales? (*Pointing to his false leg*) And is this whalebone limb not a reminder of whales? How can whales disturb them from whales?
STUBB: (*Backing away*) Sir.
AHAB: Here, man. Send everybody aft.
STUBB: Sir?
AHAB: Send everybody aft. You there at the masthead — come down!

(**STUBB** *sends* **PIP** *below. He returns with* **QUEEQUEG, ISHMAEL, DUNDEE,** *and* **STARBUCK**. *The* **SHIP'S COMPANY** *assembles on deck, with an air of expectancy. Whilst this is happening,* **AHAB** *stands with his back to them, staring out to sea*)

AHAB: (*Suddenly turning to face them*) What do ye do when ye see a whale, men?
THE CREW: Sing out for him!

AHAB: Good! And what do ye do next, men?
THE CREW: Lower away, and after him!
AHAB: Good again. Mr. Starbuck, hand me yon top-maul.

(**STARBUCK** *hands* **AHAB** *the hammer*)

Now — (*He holds up a gold coin*) — d'ye see this Spanish ounce of gold? 'Tis a sixteen dollar piece, men. D'ye see it?

(*Murmuring amongst* **THE CREW** *as* **AHAB** *goes to the main mast. He holds up the gold piece in one hand and the hammer in the other, waits for silence*)

Now. Whosoever of ye raises me a white-headed whale with a wrinkled brow and a crooked jaw — whosoever of ye raises me that white-headed whale, with three holes punctured in his starboard fluke — whosoever of ye raises me that same white whale, look ye — he shall have this gold piece, my boys.

(**THE CREW** *cheer as he nails the gold piece to the mast*)

TAHITI: Captain Ahab — that white whale must be the one that some call Moby Dick.
AHAB: (*Throwing down the hammer*) Moby Dick? Do ye know the White Whale then, Tahiti?
TAHITI: Does he fan-tail a little curious, sir, before he goes down?
MANXMAN: And has he a curious spout, too — very bushy, and mighty quick, Captain Ahab?
QUEEQUEG: And he has one, two, three — oh! a good many irons in him too, Captain — (*screwing his hand round and round*) — like, like —
AHAB: Corkscrew! Aye Queequeg, the harpoons lie all twisted and wrenched in him; aye Manxman, his spout is a big one, and as white as a pile of Nantucket wool after sheepshearing; aye Tahiti, he fantails like a split jib in a squall. It is Moby Dick ye have seen men — Moby Dick!
STARBUCK: Captain Ahab, I have heard of Moby Dick. Was it not Moby Dick that took off thy leg?
AHAB: Who told thee that?

(*Pause*)

Aye, Starbuck; aye men, it was Moby Dick that dismasted me, Moby Dick that brought me to this dead stump I stand on now. (*His voice rising with emotion*) But I'll chase him round Good Hope, and round the Horn, and round the Norway Maelstrom, and round perdition's flames before I give him up. And this is what ye have shipped for, men — to chase that white whale all over the earth till he spouts black blood. What say ye, men — will ye splice hands on it now? I think ye do look brave.
THE CREW: Aye! Aye! A sharp eye for the White Whale! A sharp lance for Moby Dick!
AHAB: God bless ye, men. Pip — go and draw the long measure of grog.

(**PIP** *goes off.* **THE CREW** *talk excitedly amongst themselves*)

But what's this long face for, Mr. Starbuck? Art thou not game for Moby Dick?

STARBUCK: I am game for his crooked jaw, and for the jaws of death too, Captain Ahab, if it fairly comes in the way of business — but I came here to hunt whales, not my commander's vengeance. How many barrels will thy vengeance yield thee, even if thou gettest it? It will not fetch thee much in our Nantucket market.

AHAB: Nantucket market! Hoot! If money's to be the measure, man, and the accountants have computed their great counting-house the globe by girdling it round with guineas, one to every three parts of an inch — then let me tell thee that my vengeance will fetch a great premium *here*. (*He smites his chest*)

STARBUCK: Vengeance on a dumb brute, that simply smote thee from blindest instinct? Madness! To be enraged with such a dumb thing, Captain Ahab, seems blasphemous.

AHAB: Hark ye, Starbuck, and look to the lower layer. All visible objects, man, appear as pasteboard masks — are dumb, unreasoning. But in each living act, some yet unknown but *reasoning* thing puts forth itself — *from out behind that mask.* If man will strike, strike through the mask! How can the prisoner reach outside except by thrusting through the wall? The White Whale is that wall, shoved near to me. Sometimes I think there's naught beyond. But to know that there *could* be — that is enough. He tasks me, he heaps me, I see in him outrageous strength, with inscrutable malice sinewing it. That inscrutable thing is chiefly what I hate — and be the White Whale agent, or the White Whale principal, I'll wreak that hate upon him. Talk not to me of blasphemy, man — I'd strike the sun if it insulted me. Who's over me? *Truth hath no confines.* Take off that doltish stare!

(**STARBUCK** *turns away.*
PIP *comes back with a flagon*)

Gather round men, and bring your lances — each man must bear a harpoon.

(*Each holding a harpoon, the* **SHIP'S COMPANY** *form a circle around him. A harpoon is handed to* **AHAB. STARBUCK** *is the last to join the circle, reluctantly.* **AHAB** *takes a swig from the flagon, passes it to* **STARBUCK**)

Drink and pass! Round with it, round! Short draughts, long swallows, men — 'tis hot as Satan's hoof. That way it went, this way it comes.

(*The flagon goes round the circle and comes back to him*)

Now then, my braves — hold your irons aloft — (*As they do so* **AHAB** *holds up his own harpoon*) — and find me with your points at the centre.

(*Each man touches the point of his harpoon against* **AHAB's**, *forming a canopy over him.* **STARBUCK** *is again reluctant — but a look from* **AHAB** *quells any rebellion*)

AHAB: (*Passing round the flagon*) Now drink again. Drink, ye harpooners — and drink, ye men that crew the dreadful whale-boat. Death to Moby Dick! God hunt us all, if we do not hunt Moby Dick to his death!

THE CREW: (*Drinking, their harpoons still held above* **AHAB**) Death to Moby Dick! God hunt us all, if we do not hunt Moby Dick to his death!

AHAB: Aye, men – who can swerve us? The path to my fixed purpose is laid with iron rails, whereon my soul is grooved to run. Naught's an obstacle, naught's an angle to the iron way!

THE CREW:(*Clashing their harpoons together*) Death to Moby Dick! Naught's an angle to the iron way!

(*The group breaks up, cheering.* **AHAB**, **STARBUCK**, *and* **STUBB** *go below.* **THE CREW** *come forward as a chorus, their harpoons still in their hands*)

THE CREW:

1.

There is a galloping in the sea
a galloping without hooves
like a tidal race
or a sea-god's heartbeat
can you hear it, Moby Dick?
and even though you hear it for the first time
it is not a beginning
(death is not a beginning)
it is not a beginning
it is the end of something

2.

Through rain-pelt and wind-lash
through hail-clunk and storm-thrust
I am coming

through gales that slash
like a butcher's knife·
and flying and flying the flag of my search
I am coming

across still seas
where no wind stirs
and my flag's as limp
as an old man's cock
I am coming

I need no flag
I *am* a flag
I am my own flag, Moby Dick

as relentless as dusk
on the heels of the daylight
forsaking firesides
and the charms of women
standing fearless and proud
as seas break over me
I am coming

I am coming, Moby Dick

and standing fearless and proud
as seas break over me
I think of your heart
and I sharpen my lance

                    3.
Now know this:
your death like a ship
is sailing towards you
I am your bad luck, Moby Dick
and I wait and I wait
as death waits
as bad luck waits
as a murderer waits
wearing a cheap suit
and leaning against a wall
I wait, Moby Dick

know this:
as you shiver in the grey waters of the Atlantic
where the crabs bite and the gulls scream over you
know this:
as you loll in the blue waters of the Pacific
where the shark's black fin is a flag on the water
that the flag of *your death* is heading towards you
it is coming, Moby Dick
as the black compass needle is drawn to the north
as the male is drawn to the female
as death is drawn towards hospitals
my lance is drawn to your heart

HOOOOOOO——————WAH! goes the line

HOOOOOOO——————WAH! goes the iron

as stout through the waves comes the prow of my
        death-ship
wherever you're hiding my quick lance shall find you
and send you spinning to a cave of blood

YOU: LANCE
my tall companion of wood and iron
sharper than a thousand razors
sharper even than my woman's tongue
come dream by my side as I lie in my hammock
o dream of his blood that you soon will be tasting

4.

Sometimes a day goes down for no reason
like milk curdling in winter
like fresh-caught fish stinking
like new-poured wine tasting of dust and decay

on days like these
I prowl the deck and I stare at the ocean
or I lie in my hammock and think of my woman
I think of the day that we walked by the shoreline
and *you* stirred in me for the first time
and I gripped her hand like a lance and drew blood
and she screamed and she screamed
and she screamed in my face
but my hand went on tightening
and she went on screaming
I will pay you back for that scream, Moby Dick

5.

(For six individual voices: **a, b, c, d, e,** *&* **f.)**

a: I hate white as a colour
b: it's a nothing, a zero
c: I can't tell what it's thinking
d: it's too indistinct

a: I hate white as a colour
b: it's like someone who's vanished
c: ˙or a house that's left empty
d: or a glass with no drink

a: I hate white as a colour
b: is it plotting against me?
c: I don't like its silence
d: or the way it won't speak

a: I hate white as a colour
b: like a ship with no sailors
c: there's something about it
d: that gives me the creeps

e: like snow, miles of it, all silent
f: or a blind man's eye, all white, with no pupil
ALL: it gives me the creeps, I tell you

a: I can see black as it moves towards me
b: I can see black as it turns, and moves away from me
c&d: I can see black

as it stays still
and waits
for me to approach it

e: but what does white do?
f: where is the edge of it   **a:**   does it have an edge?
b: where is the centre of it **c:**   does it have a centre?
d: is it moving or not?

e: like snow, miles of it, all silent
f: or a blind man's eye, all white, with no pupil
ALL: it gives me the creeps, I tell you

6.

Now I say this
I am a man, I suffer
I suffer from the world and from women
I suffer from hopes that have died on my tongue
I suffer from words I have bit back and swallowed
they have stuck in my gut and bred there, like rats
gnawing my gut with a certain sharpness
and swearing, and spitting, and fighting amongst
        themselves

these rats hate you, Moby Dick
at the sound of your name they tense and grow silent
and pain stabs my gut as they mass in a ball
a grey heavy ball, the ball of my hatred
and I reach down inside me and touch it and stroke it
and I bring it still blinking up into the light

and I hold my hatred in my hand, and I weigh it
and I roll it, silent, in the palm of my hand
and I mould it, stealthy, to the shape of my hand

and I pick up my lance, and my hatred holds it
and I measure the distance from it to the target
and my lance is THROWN

           but my hatred stays with me
it stays in my hand, like my skin, always waiting
like my skin, like my shadow, it always stays with me

it is here now, waiting: for you, Moby Dick

[7.

Your silence insults me
your whiteness insults me
your great size insults me

you insult me, Moby Dick
you are not me, that insults me
worst of all, your absence insults me
it is true, this
you are not me, Moby Dick
I call you to face me
but you don't, you are missing
I am here all the time
then it is war between us
a war between presence and absence
you are all the things I have ever hated
you are not me, Moby Dick
you think you are innocent, nothing is innocent
everything is separate, everything is war
my ship is a country, with its own flag flying
my ship is my country, you are not my country
my country is this ship, you are not this country
you insult this country
by your silence
by your whiteness
by your bigness
by your presence
by your absence
by everything about you
you are not me, Moby Dick]

8

ISHMAEL ALONE:

On a white sea
beneath a white stone sky
my ship floats, ringed round
by the white walls of my hatred
and you are the door, Moby Dick

(*Lights fade to black*)

FOUR : THE SPIRIT SPOUT

(*Moonlight.*
ISHMAEL *on deck. Behind him,* **AHAB** *and the* **SHIP'S COMPANY** *perform the scene in mime*)

ISHMAEL: Weeks passed, and under easy sail
the Pequod slowly swept across the water-globe
into the South Atlantic. And there,
upon a night when all the waves rolled by
like silver scrolls — on this same night,

far in advance of us, a silvery jet was seen.
Lit by the moon, it seemed celestial:
as if some plumed and glittering god
had rose up from the sea.

(*A jet of water is seen, then disappears*)

Ahab gave word that all the sails be set,
and then with every masthead manned
the craft rolled down before the wind.
Filling the hollows of so many sails,
the breeze transformed the rushing deck
to air beneath our feet — the ship seemed bound
for heaven, yet still ploughed on, ever and ever drawn
towards that spout, its horizontal goal.
Ahab continually paced; his one live leg
made echoes on the deck, whilst from his deadened limb
came a reply just like a coffin tap —
on life and death this old man walked.
But though the ship so swiftly sped, and though
from every eye, like arrows, eager glances shot,
the silvery jet was seen no more that night.
Each sailor swore that he had seen it once,
but not a second time.
                                This midnight spout
had almost been forgot, when lo!
some three nights later, at a similar hour
it was observed again —

(*The jet appears again, from a different part of the stage*)

but though the ship once more gave chase
it vanished into air.
                                Night after night,
the same: jetting mysterious
out of the moonlit sea ahead of us
this solitary spout

(*The jet appears again*)

forever lured us on.

(*The wind begins to increase, slowly building throughout the next passage*)

We turned eastward
towards the Cape. The winds began to howl.
In the grey seas close to our bows, strange forms
darted about, whilst to our stern there flapped
gigantic flocks of sea-ravens, inscrutable.

Cape of Good Hope? More like
the Cape of Hope Abandoned — purgatory,
inhabited by souls transformed to fish or birds,
condemned to swim on everlastingly
or beat their wings against the blackened air
which stretched without horizon.
The gales increased. With all secured aloft
we roped ourselves onto the rail, and stood
like sailors made of wax as seas broke over us.
Ahab for hours and hours would stand
gazing to windward. Day after day
the ship tore on, braving the madness of the waves.
But ever calm, milk-white, unwavering,
shooting its feathered fountain to the sky
and beckoning, still beckoning, the solitary jet

(*The jet appears again*)

would often-times be seen.

Nor could Starbuck forget the sight
of Ahab, when, going below one night,
he glanced into his cabin, and beheld
the old man sleeping in his screwed-down chair,

(*Lights up on* **AHAB** *in his cabin,* **STARBUCK** *standing by the door*)

rain-soaked, a lantern swinging from his fist.
And though his body sat erect, his head
was forward thrown, so that his sleeping eyes
were fixed, and ever fixed, upon the chart.

STARBUCK: Terrible old man! Sleeping in this gale, and still thou steadfastly eyes thy purpose.

(*The wind gradually dies down*)

FIVE : STUBB KILLS A WHALE

(*A clear, bright day.*
AHAB *and* **SHIP'S COMPANY** *on deck. Above, keeping look-out,*
QUEEQUEG)

STARBUCK: Fine weather, praise the Lord.

(**AHAB** *comes to stand beside him*)

Storm's gone off to leeward, sir.
AHAB: (*Staring out to sea*) Aye.

(*Pause*)

Then why should the pain in this crushed leg not go off also, when 'tis so long dissolved? (*Turning to* **STARBUCK**) But mayest thou not feel the fiery pains of hell forever, and without a body?
STARBUCK: Me, sir?
AHAB: Not *thou*, Starbuck — thou hast naught to fear from hell's flames, thy cold stare will freeze them over. *Mankind* I meant, man.
STARBUCK: But with faith, sir —
AHAB: Faith? Faith feeds among the tombs like a jackal.

(*Pause*)

STARBUCK: Faith — is no jackal, sir. Without faith, Captain Ahab —
AHAB: Aye, well?
STARBUCK: Without *faith*, sir, we live in meaning as fish live in water — without recognition, blind. 'Tis a rock, sir, a rock —
AHAB: But in a gale, is't not better to risk perishing in the howling infinite than be dashed upon the rock — even if that rock were safety itself?
STARBUCK: (*Doesn't answer*)
AHAB: What d' ye reach for, Starbuck? Your own hands, is it? (*Takes one of* **STARBUCK'S** *hands*) Is this all ye grasp? Reach further, man. (*Pointing*) Out there, *beyond yourself*.

(*A pause, and then a sudden shout from the masthead*)

QUEEQUEG: There she blows! There! There! There!
AHAB: Where away?
QUEEQUEG: On the lee beam, two miles off — a school of them!

(*Commotion on deck /* **QUEEQUEG** *descends*)

AHAB: What colour, man.
QUEEQUEG: Like sea-coal, sir — grey-black.
AHAB: 'Tis your whale, Mr. Stubb. Look to the ship, Mr. Starbuck. (*Goes below*)

(*The boat is lowered into the water.* **QUEEQUEG, ISHMAEL, DUNDEE,** *and* **MANXMAN** *are at the oars,* **STUBB** *at the helm. They row furiously towards the whale*)

STUBB: (*Perfectly calm*) It's against my religion to get mad, but — pull, won't ye? Come on, why don't some of ye burst a blood vessel? Who's been dropping an anchor overboard — we don't budge an inch, we're becalmed. Hallo, there's grass growing in the bottom of the boat. This won't do, boys — the short and long of it is, men — will ye spit fire or not?

(*They are now near the whale*)

Easy now, easy — keep cool, keep cool boys, cucumbers is the word. Stand up, Queequeg — now, give it to him!

(**QUEEQUEG** *throws the harpoon. They pull on the line, which goes tight.* **QUEEQUEG** *hurls dart after dart at the whale, retrieving each time to throw again. Meanwhile, the whale is held secure by the whale-line. There is a sudden splash of blood, then an outburst of cheering from* **THE CREW**)

ISHMAEL: As darkness fell, we towed the whale back to the ship — followed by hundreds on hundreds of sharks, all determined to gorge themselves on the dead leviathan.

(*The boat arrives back at the ship. It is now dark. The action is mimed during the following speech*)

ISHMAEL: And whilst the whale was being secured to the ship's side, and all through that long night whilst the blubber was being cut from him — for all the world like the rind from a giant orange — all through that night Queequeg and the Manxman kept up an incessant murdering of sharks — who viciously snapped, not only at the whale, but also at each other's disembowelments, sometimes even turning round to bite at their own bodies, into such a frenzy had they been driven by the smell of blood.
STUBB: A steak, a steak before I sleep. You, Queequeg — overboard you go and cut me one from his small.

(**QUEEQUEG** *does so, re-emerges with the steak, takes it below, then comes back and resumes his work*)

STUBB: (*Pacing about the deck*) Hey, cook! Hurry it up there, cook!

(**PIP** *brings up the cooked steak, gives it to* **STUBB**, *begins to go off*)

STUBB: (*Tastes it*) Hey, cook — sail this way, cook.

(**PIP** *comes back reluctantly*)

Now, cook — don't you think this steak is rather overdone? You've been beating it too much, cook — it's too tender. Them sharks now — don't you see they like it tough and rare? What a shindy they're kicking up! Go and talk to 'em, cook, and tell them to behave more civilly. Here, take this lantern, and go preach to 'em.
PIP: (*Going to the side with the lantern*) Fellow-critters — stop that damn noise, d' ye hear? Stop that damn —
STUBB: Cook, cook — you mustn't swear like that when you're preaching, that's no way to convert sinners. Talk to 'em gentlemanly.
PIP: Now look here, sharks, you must govern that wicked nature of yours. You are sharks, certain — but if you govern the shark in you, why then you'll be angels — for angels are nothing more than sharks well-governed.

STUBB: Well done, Pip — that's Christianity. Go on.

PIP: Ain't no use, Mr. Stubb — them sharks just keep on biting and slapping.

STUBB: Give them the benediction then, and I'll return to my supper.

PIP: Cussed fellow-critters! Kick up the damnedest row as ever you can, fill your damn bellies till they burst — and then die.

STUBB: Well done, cook — now, stand here and pay attention.

PIP: (*Unwillingly*) All attention.

STUBB: Now — how old are you, Pip?

PIP: Don't know, sir.

STUBB: Don't know when you were born? Still, no matter — because you'll have to go and be born all over again — you don't know how to cook a whale-steak yet, d' ye see? Here, taste this.

PIP: (*Tasting the steak*) Best cooked steak I ever tasted. Juicy, very very juicy.

STUBB: Cook, do you belong to the church?

PIP: (*Sullen*) Passed one in Cape Town once.

STUBB: And where d'ye expect to go when you die, hah?

PIP: Up there.

STUBB: Up to the top of the mast, eh cook? Be pretty cold, won't you?

PIP: (*Doesn't answer*)

STUBB: (*Swallowing the last of the steak*) Well now, cook — this steak of yours was so bad that I've had to get it out of sight as soon as possible, see? And in future, when you cook another whale-steak for my private table here, don't spoil it by over-doing — hold the steak in one hand, and show a live coal to it with the other — and then dish it, d' ye hear?

(**PIP** *nods, still sullen*)

Now, away you sail.

(**PIP** *turns to go*)

Halloa, stop! Make a bow before you go.

(**PIP** *turns and bows, then starts to go off*)

And cook — (**PIP** *stops*) — whale-balls for breakfast, don't forget.

(**PIP** *nods, his back to* **STUBB**, *then starts to go off again*)

And cook? (**PIP** *stops*) Don't forget to say your prayers now, cook.

PIP: (*Going off finally*) Wish that damn whale would eat him instead of him eat it. I'm blessed if he ain't more of a shark than old King Shark himself.

(*Dawn.*
The whale's head is hoisted over the side and hangs suspended over the deck.
  AHAB *comes up from below*)

AHAB: (*Stares at the head for some moments before speaking*) Speak, mighty head, and tell us the secret that is within thee. Of all divers, thou hast dived the deepest.

Where unrecorded names and navies rust, where in her murderous hold this frigate earth is ballasted with millions of the drowned — there, in that awful water-land, was thy familiar home. Thou saw'st the locked lovers when they lept from their flaming ship — true to each other, when heaven seemed false to them. Thou hast been where bell and diver never went, hast slept by many a sailor's side — where sleepless mothers nightly pray to lay them down. O head! Thou hast seen enough to split the planets, and not one syllable is thine!

DUNDEE: (*From the masthead*) Sail ho!

AHAB: Aye? Well now, that's cheering. That lively cry upon this deadly calm might almost convert a better man. Where away?

DUNDEE: Three points on the starboard bow, sir, and bringing down her breeze to us.

AHAB: Better and better, man. Would that St. Paul would come along that way, and blow upon *my* breezelessness — eh, Mr. Starbuck?

SIX : THE JEROBOAM'S STORY

(**AHAB**, **STARBUCK**, *and* **DUNDEE** *on deck*)

STARBUCK: (*Peering over the side*) The Jeroboam, out of Nantucket. They're lowering a boat, sir.

AHAB: Ahoy, Mayhew! Hast seen the White Whale?

STARBUCK: He's got a flag up — quarantine.

DUNDEE: 'Tis a plague ship.

AHAB: Quiet, man.

(*A boat comes into view. In it are* **CAPTAIN MAYHEW** *of the Jeroboam,* **GABRIEL**, *and* **ANOTHER OARSMAN**)

The White Whale — hast thou seen him?

MAYHEW: Seen him, aye. (*To the oarsman*) No further.

AHAB: I fear not thy epidemic, man.

GABRIEL: Think of the fevers, yellow and billious! Beware of the horrible plague!

MAYHEW: Gabriel, Gabriel! Thou must either — (*His voice trails off*)

AHAB: (*Impatient*)What of the White Whale?

GABRIEL: Think of thy whale-boat, stoven and sunk! Beware of the horrible tail!

MAYHEW: I tell thee again, Gabriel — (*His voice trails off*)

AHAB: Mayhew!

MAYHEW: Last year it was. South of the Japanese ground. My chief mate, Kingdom, insisted on lowering for him. Whereupon this fellow, who calls himself after the archangel —

GABRIEL: Not calls, who *is* the archangel.

MAYHEW: Who calls himself after the archangel, and has my crew in thrall — this fellow ascends the masthead and calls down prophecies of speedy doom on all who would —

GABRIEL: (*Pointing downwards*) Think of the blasphemer — *dead*, down there! Think of the blasphemer's end!

MAYHEW: And so it proved — before my mate could try his lance, a broad white shadow rose up from the deep and smote him into the air for a distance of about fifty yards. Not a chip of the boat was harmed, nor a hair of any oarsman's head, but Kingdom forever sank.

GABRIEL: Think not to touch that holiness, or follow the blasphemer!

AHAB: The Devil take thee! (*To* **STARBUCK**) Starbuck, look through the letter bag. (*To* **MAYHEW**) Captain, I believe we have letter here for one of your officers.

STARBUCK: (*Taking out a letter*) 'Tis but a dim scrawl, a woman's hand — the man's wife, I'll wager. Aye — Mr. Harry Kingdom, ship Jeroboam. (*Giving it to* **AHAB**) Why it's Kingdom, and he's dead!

MAYHEW: Poor fellow! And from his wife — but let me have it.

GABRIEL: (*To* **AHAB**) Nay, keep it thyself — thou art soon going that way.

AHAB: Curses throttle thee! Captain Mayhew, stand by now to receive it.

(*He takes a harpoon, fastens the letter onto the tip, and holds it out to the boat. As* **MAYHEW** *reaches for it,* **GABRIEL** *intercepts and throws it back towards* **AHAB**. *It lands in the water*)

GABRIEL: See how 'tis now safely delivered.

MAYHEW: Gabriel, I —

GABRIEL: (*To the* **OARSMAN**) Give way, and back to the ship!

(*A wave breaks, the boat is gone*)

STARBUCK: (*To* **AHAB**) Shall I retrieve the letter, sir?

(**AHAB** *looks at him, goes.*
The letter floats in the water)

SEVEN : THE CASTAWAY

(**ISHMAEL**, *his hand bandaged.*
Behind him, the scene is performed in mime — **STUBB**, **QUEEQUEG**, **PIP**, **DUNDEE**, **TAHITI**)

ISHMAEL: It so happened that Stubb's after-oarsman sprained his hand — and, temporarily, Pip was put into his place. The first time the boat paddled upon the whale, Pip showed much nervousness; and when the fish, on receiving Queequeg's darted iron, gave a rap with its tail right under Pip's seat, he lept, paddle in hand, out of the boat — and in such a way that part of the whale-line became entangled about him. In less than half a minute, this entire thing happened.

STUBB: Damn him, cut!

(**QUEEQUEG** *cuts the line*)

ISHMAEL: And so the whale was lost and Pip was saved.

STUBB: Stick to the boat, Pip. If you jump again, I won't pick you up, mind that. We can't afford to lose whales by the likes of you. A whale would sell for thirty times what you would, Pip, in Alabama.

ISHMAEL: But we are all in the hands of the gods, and Pip jumped again. But this time he did not breast out the line — and hence, when the whale started to run, Pip was left behind on the sea, a lonely castaway.

(*Behind* **ISHMAEL,** *only* **PIP'S** *head is now visible in the water*)

By the merest chance, the ship at last rescued him — but from that hour Pip went about the deck an idiot — such, at least, they said he was. The sea had kept his body up, but drowned the infinite of his soul. Not drowned entirely, though. Rather — carried it down alive to wondrous depths, where strange shapes of the primal world floated before his sea-drenched eyes. He saw God's hand upon the lever of the tides, and spoke it — and so men called him mad. But Pip paid them no heed, for celestial thought wanders far from mortal reason, and is indifferent to it — as indifferent as God is, perhaps.

(**PIP** *stands behind* **ISHMAEL,** *looking past him. He is soaking wet*)

PIP: Funny how everyone's a sheer drop, eh Captain? Like the drop of the ocean from the top to the bottom. Ye get dizzy when you look down.

(*Pause/he peers down*)

On the floor of the ocean there's a mark in the sand. In the shape of a man, but I can't make him out. Or perhaps it's a ship. Funny what the sea covers up, eh Captain? The waves are just the top of it. They go *over* all the rest, don't they?

EIGHT : STOWING DOWN AND CLEARING UP

(**SHIP'S COMPANY** *on deck.*
Supervised by **STARBUCK** *and* **STUBB,** **THE CREW** *bring large pieces of the whale's blanket onto the deck and chop them up, then feed them into the try-works — a dull red glow offstage. The impression should be one of hot, dirty, physicality — and of work which is highly dangerous.*
During the chopping up of the blanket, the following work-song is sung, accompanied by a slow, rhythmic beat)

QUEEQUEG AND CREW:
                         I don't want no long tall captain
                         oh he too mean, Lord, oh he too mean
                         (*repeat*)

When he shout, he sound like thunder
up in the clouds, Lord, up in the clouds
(*repeat*)

Got my harpoon, it shine like silver
in my right hand, Lord, in my right hand
(*repeat*)

When you meet my long tall captain
just bow your head, Lord, just bow your head
(*repeat*)

Don't want no sugar in my coffee
it make me mean, Lord, it make me mean
(*repeat*)

(*The tune changes. The rhythm quickens, gradually becoming more frenzied*)

Well very early in the morning (early, well-a)
well very early in the morning (early, well-a)
very early in the morning (well-a)
very early when I rise

Well I find you beside me (find you, well-a)
well I find you beside me (find you, well-a)
yes I find you beside me (well-a)
by my right side

Well you shine like silver (silver, well-a)
well you shine like silver (silver, well-a)
yes you shine like silver (well-a)
but you sharper than a knife

Well some say you're a razor (razor, well-a)
yes some say you're a razor (razor, well-a)
but I say you're a killer (well-a)
going to take his life

[Going to kill him with my weapon (kill him, well-a)
going to kill him with my weapon (kill him, well-a)
yes going to kill him with my weapon (well-a)
going to kill him in the fight

Going to chop him all to pieces (chop him, well-a)
going to take him to the fire (fire, well-a)
going to burn him in the fire (well-a)
till he blaze up in the night

Going to blaze up in the darkness (blaze up, well-a)
going to blaze up in the darkness (blaze up, well-a)
yes going to blaze up in the darkness (well-a)
going to give me light]

(After the whale has been fed into the try-works, the resulting oil is poured into huge casks which are rolled down the hatch to be stored in the ship's hold — this can be represented very simply, using a single cask. The deck is then cleared of all the tools that have been used in the scene, hosed down, and thoroughly scrubbed clean. During this operation the mood gradually becomes more and more light-hearted: as the work comes to an end, **THE CREW** *go off one by one and come back wearing clean clothes; they link arms in two's and three's and stroll around the deck.*
STUBB, *having changed his clothes, pretends to admire himself in a mirror)*

DUNDEE: (*Approaching* **STUBB**) The oil's safely stowed in the hold, sir.
STUBB: Oil? Did you say oil? Nasty, sticky stuff — smells like the left wing of the Day of Judgement. Canst thou not see we've just this minute got this parlour clean — and thou comest to me with thy 'oil'? Speak to me of sofas, man, or afternoon teas, or napkins. Anything but — there now, I've forgotten the word. What shade of carpet shall we have for the deck, d' ye think?
DUNDEE: (*Stares at him*) Carpet, sir? But when the whales —
STUBB: Wales? Is that where ye come from? I knew it was one of them tiny, rain-soaked countries. Or — (*seizing* **DUNDEE** *by the ear*) — speakest thou of the sound ye shall make when I twist your ear — thus?

(**DUNDEE** *lets out a roar,* **STUBB** *lets go of him*)

Away with your wails, man! (*Looking down*) I think I see a spot of soot on the deck there. (*Back to* **DUNDEE**) Away, and bring us napkins!

(*As* **DUNDEE** *goes off,* **AHAB** *comes up on deck*)

Here comes the old man, or it's somebody else, that's certain. (*Looks round*) It is the old man — and with a face on him like a squall coming up. Oh well, it'll pass off soon enough — everything passes off at sea. And if it doesn't, it's no matter.

NINE : THE DOUBLOON

(*On the deck, the outline of the doubloon.*
AHAB *enters, goes to examine it*)

AHAB: Three peaks of the Andes: on one a flame, a tower on another, on the third a crowing cock. And round them in a ring, the zodiac. The firm tower here, that is Ahab; the fiery volcano, that is Ahab; the valiant and undaunted cock, that too is Ahab. And now he enters the sign of storms, the equinox — right opposite … another equinox, at Aries. From storm to storm. So be it, then. (*Smites his chest*) Here's stout stuff for woe to work on. (*Goes*)

(**STARBUCK** *comes foward, stops in front of the doubloon*)

STARBUCK: Some devil's work. And yet … a dark valley between three heavenly peaks — the Trinity, perhaps. So in this vale of death, *God* girds us round; and over all the sun still reigns — our beacon and our hope. And yet the great sun is no fixture — for seek his warmth at midnight and ye gaze for him in vain! This coin speaks wise and true, but — sadly still. Enough. Sometimes the truth can shake you falsely. (*Goes*)

(**STUBB** *comes forward*)

STUBB: First the old man and now Starbuck — both with faces to a depth of nine fathoms. What's here. The zodiac — the life of man in twelve chapters! To begin, there's Aries, the ram — lecherous dog, he begets us. Then Taurus, the bull — he bumps us into life. Then comes Gemini, the twins — that's vice and virtue. We try to reach virtue, when lo! along comes Cancer the crab, and drags us back — right into the path of: Leo, a roaring lion, who gives us a few fierce dabs with his paw. We escape into the arms of: Virgo, the virgin, that's our first love. We marry and think we'll be happy forever, but then along comes Libra, the scales — happiness weighed and found wanting. And while we are feeling sad about that — lo! we suddenly jump, because Scorpio, the scorpion, has stung us in the rear. We are busy curing the wound when whang come the arrows — Sagittarius, the archer, is amusing himself. And as we pluck out the shafts, look out, here comes the battering ram — Capricorn, the goat, rushing full tilt — and tosses us headlong. Whereupon Aquarius pours out his whole deluge and drowns us, and we wind up with Pisces, the fishes, and that's where we sleep. There's a sermon now, written in high heaven, and the sun goes through it every year, all alive and hearty. And why not? What's good for the sun is good enough for Stubb. The best way through toil and trouble is to … (*Turns a cartwheel*) … *turn cartwheels* through them. *Jolly's* the word, I tell ye. (*Goes*)

(**MANXMAN** *comes forward*)

MANXMAN: If the White Whale be raised, it must be in a month and a day, when the sun is in one of these signs. I've studied signs, and know their marks — they were taught me years ago, by the old witch in Copenhagen. Now. In what sign will the sun be then? (*Examines the doubloon*) So this is the way the ship goes, is it? This way at last? (*Goes*)

(**PIP** *comes forward*)

PIP: (*Examines the doubloon*) Here's the ship's navel, and they're all on fire to unscrew it. But unscrew your navel, and what's the consequence? But if it stays here, then that's ugly too — for when aught's nailed to the mast, it's a sure sign that things grow desperate. Ha! Ha! Old Ahab! The White Whale — he'll nail ye! This is a pine tree. My father cut down a pine tree once, and found a silver ring grown over in it, some old darkey's wedding ring. How did it get there? And so they'll say in the resurrection, when they come to fish up this old mast and find a doubloon lodged in it, with bedded oysters for the bark. Oh, the gold! The precious,

precious gold! The green miser'll hoard ye soon! Hish! Hish! God goes among the worlds blackberrying. Cook! Ho, cook — and cook us! Jenny! Hey, hey, hey, hey, hey, Jenny! Jenny! Jenny get your hoe-cake done! (*Goes*)

(**TAHITI** *comes forward, bends over the outline of the doubloon. He reaches down and touches the side of it, as if to give it a push. The doubloon begins to spin. It gradually gathers speed, becoming a circle of pure light*)

TEN : LEG AND ARM

(**AHAB** *and* **STUBB**, *both looking overboard*)

STUBB: English — by his brass buttons.

(**CAPTAIN BOOMER** *and* **JACK BUNGER** *climb over the side*)

AHAB: Hast seen the White Whale?
BOOMER: (*Showing his empty sleeve*) See you this? (*Holding out his other hand*) Boomer, ship Samuel Enderby, out of London.
AHAB: (*Taking the empty sleeve instead*) Nay my hearty, let us shake empty bones together. An arm that can never shrink, and a leg that can never run. Where didst thou see the White Whale — how long ago?
BOOMER: The White Whale. (*Pointing*) There I saw him, on the Line, last season.
AHAB: And he took that arm off, did he?
BOOMER: Aye, he was the cause of it — and that leg, too?
AHAB: Spin me the yarn. How was it?
BOOMER: It was the first time I ever cruised on the Line. I was ignorant of the White Whale at that time. Well, one day we lowered for a pod of four or five whales, and my boat fastened to one of them — when up from the bottom of the sea comes this bouncing great leviathan, with a milk-white head and hump, all crows' feet and wrinkles, and harpoons sticking in his starboard fluke.
AHAB: Aye, they were mine — my irons. But on!
BOOMER: (*Good humouredly*) Give me a chance then. Well this old grandfather, with the white head and hump, runs all afoam into the pod, and goes to snapping at my line.
AHAB: Aye — wanted to free the fast fish — an old trick.
BOOMER: Then turns, d' ye see, my line in his jaw, and brings us onto his starboard fluke, where my arm met with one of your irons, and — . A devilish wound it was, and had this good doctor here — (by the way, Captain — Jack Bunger, ship's surgeon: Bunger, the Captain) — had this doctor not sat up all night with me drinking hot rum toddies —
BUNGER: (*To* **AHAB**) The Captain, sir, is apt to be facetious — he knows that as a strict abstinence man — en passant, as the French remark — I never touch a drop —
BOOMER: Of water! He can't touch it, throws him into fits.
BUNGER: Laughing fits, coughing fits, sneezing fits —
BOOMER: What a rogue is this Bunger, Captain, I tell you —

AHAB: What became of the White Whale?

BOOMER: The Whale?

AHAB: Did'st cross his wake again?

BOOMER: Aye, twice.

AHAB: But could not fasten?

BOOMER: Didn't try — ain't one limb enough? There would be great glory in killing him, I know that — but he's best left alone, is the White Whale — don't you think so, Captain?

AHAB: He is. But what is best left alone, that accursed thing is always what most allures. He's all a magnet! How long since thou saw him last? Which way heading?

BUNGER: (*Walking around* **AHAB**) Bless my soul and curse the foul fiend's — this man's blood — it's at boiling point!

AHAB: (*Pushing him away*) Avast! (*To* **BOOMER**) Which way heading?

BOOMER: Good God. What's the matter? East, I think.

AHAB: East.

BOOMER: (*Aside, to* **STUBB**) Is your Captain crazy?

(**STUBB** *puts one finger to his lip as* **AHAB** *turns away*)

BOOMER: (*To* **AHAB**) Sir?

(*But* **AHAB** *is gone - back to his cabin, to pore over the chart*)

ELEVEN : LEAKS IN LEAKS

(**AHAB** *in his cabin, examining the chart*)

AHAB: (*Hearing* **STARBUCK'S** *footsteps*) Who's there! Begone!

STARBUCK: Captain Ahab mistakes: it is I. We must heave-to — the oil is leaking, sir. We must break out the main hold and bring up the barrels.

AHAB: (*Turning*) Heave-to and break out? Now that we are nearing Japan? Heave-to for a week to tinker a parcel of old hoops?

STARBUCK: Either that sir, or waste in a day more oil than we may make good in a year. What we have come twenty thousand miles to get is worth saving, sir.

AHAB: So it is, so it is — if we get it.

STARBUCK: I was speaking of the oil in the hold, sir.

AHAB: And I was not speaking of that at all. Begone! Let it leak! The world is full of leaks. Those leaky casks are in a leaky ship. I'm all aleak myself. Aye, leaks in leaks! Yet I don't stop to plug my leak — and how could I, in this life's howling gale? Eh, Starbuck? I'll not heave-to.

STARBUCK: But what will the owners say, sir?

AHAB: Let the owners stand on Nantucket beach and outyell the typhoons. Owners? Thou art always prating to me, Starbuck, about those miserly owners — as if the owners were my conscience. But look ye, the only real owner of a thing is its commander — on deck!

STARBUCK: (*Advancing nervously*) One better than I would overlook in thee what he might resent in a younger man — aye, and in a happier, Captain Ahab.

AHAB: Dost thou dare to think critically of me? On deck!

STARBUCK: (*Still nervous*) Nay sir, not yet — I do entreat — shall we not understand each other better, Captain Ahab? (*Sits in the other chair. Then, slowly*) What is it you are seeking — into what darkness are you taking this ship?

AHAB: Not into darkness, Starbuck, but into white. Into whiteness, there are we headed.

(*A pause, then* **AHAB** *suddenly seizes a musket, points it at* **STARBUCK**)

There is but one God that is Lord over the earth, and one Captain that is lord over the Pequod — on deck!

(*A pause, then* **STARBUCK** *rises, backs away*)

STARBUCK: Thou hast outraged, not insulted me, sir. (*Pausing by the door*) I ask thee not to beware of Starbuck, for thou wouldst laugh — but let Ahab beware of Ahab. Beware of thyself, old man. (*Goes*)

AHAB: He waxes brave, but still obeys — most careful bravery, that! Ahab beware of Ahab — there's something there!

(*He paces the cabin, then puts down the musket; goes on deck, stands behind* **STARBUCK**)

STARBUCK: (*Not turning round*) I am not a ship's bell, that you can ring me, Captain Ahab.

AHAB: But something has the ringing of you, as the White Whale has the ringing of me. (*Then, quietly*) Thou art too good a fellow, Starbuck. (*Louder, to* **THE CREW**) Furl the top-gallant sails and close-reef the topsails, fore and aft. Then heave-to, and break out the main hold.

(**THE CREW** *obey*)

TWELVE : QUEEQUEG IN HIS COFFIN

(*Moonlight.*
On deck, **ISHMAEL**. *To one side, lying down,* **QUEEQUEG**. *Also on deck, watching, are* **DUNDEE**, **MANXMAN**, *and* **TAHITI**)

ISHMAEL: It was whilst the casks were being brought out of the hold — which had us sailors crawling like lizards amid much slime and dampness in the bowels of the ship — that Queequeg caught a chill, which soon lapsed into a fever; until, after several days suffering, we laid him in his hammock, very close to the door of death. Not a man of the crew but gave him up, and as for Queequeg himself —

QUEEQUEG: Ishmael.

(**ISHMAEL** *goes to him, holds his hand*)

Don't bury me in a hammock, as food for sharks.

(*Pause*)

In your country I have seen sailors who die ... laid in small canoes of dark wood ... and then be put into caves in the earth. Let me be laid in this same canoe, and then be put into the ocean, and so follow sea-paths to the heavens.
ISHMAEL: (*Turns away*) And so a coffin was ordered to be made.

> (**MANXMAN** *takes* **QUEEQUEG'S** *measurements, goes off*)

DUNDEE: Poor fellow — he'll have to die now.

> (**ISHMAEL, DUNDEE,** *and* **TAHITI** *sit down to play cards. Every so often*
> **ISHMAEL** *glances across at* **QUEEQUEG**.
> *Off, the sound of hammering as* **MANXMAN** *sings the tune (not the words) of*
> *'Where We Sail'*[1])

ISHMAEL: (*As* **DUNDEE** *lays down a card*) Why did you do that?
DUNDEE: Because I'm stupid. I prefer it that way. Intelligence frightens me. So many nice, intelligent people doing nice, intelligent things. Look what a mess it's got the world into.

> (*Pause/they continue playing.*
> **DUNDEE** *shudders*)

ISHMAEL: What is it?
DUNDEE: My overcoat, hanging up in the wardrobe at home. What if the moths get at it? Well, no matter.

> (*Pause/they continue playing*)

I keep thinking there's something coming towards me, a shape but it's got no shape, and it's got no colour and I can't hear it. And it keeps on coming and coming, and suddenly it's coming past me, all of it, and I'm in the middle of it and I can't see anything — I can't touch it or smell it but I know it's there. All around me, it's there. And then it goes. And gradually, gradually, I forget all about it. I just forget all about it, till the next time.

> (*Pause*)

ISHMAEL: So what you worried about, if you can't see it?
DUNDEE: I can see it.

> (*Pause*)

I *can* see it.
ISHMAEL: Can you see it now?
DUNDEE: (*Doesn't answer*)
ISHMAEL: Is it here now?

DUNDEE: I'm not worried about seeing it, I'm worried about forgetting it. *Why do I keep forgetting it?*

> (*Off, the singing and hammering stop.*
> **MANXMAN** *comes back carrying a coffin; with him are* **STUBB** *and* **STARBUCK**. *Hovering behind them,* **PIP**.
> *The game of cards comes to an end*)

PIP: Ha ha ha said the laughing man
Boo hoo hoo said the man who cried

Bang bang bang went the knocking man
But who spoke loudest was the man who died

> (**QUEEQUEG** *motions that he wants to be lifted into the coffin. They gently do so*)

QUEEQUEG: (*Now lying full length in the coffin*) Harpoon.

> (**ISHMAEL** *fetches* **QUEEQUEG'S** *harpoon, lays it beside him in the coffin*)

Water.

> (**DUNDEE** *goes off, brings back a flask of water, puts it in the coffin*)

Biscuits.

> (**MANXMAN** *goes off, brings back biscuits and places them in the coffin*)

Pillow.

> (**ISHMAEL** *takes off his jacket, rolls it up, places it under* **QUEEQUEG'S** *head*)

Close the hatch.

> (*The coffin lid is closed, leaving only* **QUEEQUEG'S** *head in view.*
> *Pause*)

It is enough. (*Closes his eyes*)

> (**PIP** *comes slowly up to the coffin*)

PIP: A horse went galloping
over the sea.
Under his hooves
the moon was shining.

Gallop, gallop, went the horse.
Shine, shine, went the moon.

> A horse is a shining thing.
> Over the sky
> the moon goes galloping.
> Shine, shine, my moon-horse.

(A pause, then all exit except **ISHMAEL**, *who sits alone by the coffin. The lights fade down, leaving only the coffin and* **ISHMAEL** *illuminated. A further pause, then the coffin lid opens and* **QUEEQUEG'S** *head emerges)*

QUEEQUEG: Not ready to die yet. Have left a little business unfinished.
ISHMAEL: (*Amazed*) But ... can you decide, when to die?
QUEEQUEG: (*Impatiently*) Of course. (*Getting out of the coffin*) If a man want to die, nothing can save him. If a man want to live ... only a god can kill him.

(He stretches himself, picks up his harpoon)

Now ready to fight. Now ready for Moby Dick.
ISHMAEL: (*Joyfully*) It's a miracle.

*(***TAHITI*** comes out of the darkness)*

TAHITI: Everything's a miracle. Death's a miracle. If I sliced your head off and you vanished into thin air, wouldn't that be a miracle?

THIRTEEN : THE GILDER

(A calm day.
SHIP'S COMPANY *on deck.*
This scene should have a lazy, sensual quality — everyone except **AHAB** *should appear half-asleep)*

ISHMAEL AND CREW : Pacific
you dream-rocked ocean
sea-cradle of the sinking stars
where mermen's children fall asleep
inside the hollows of the waves
which purr
and purr
and ever rub themselves
against the belly of our ship
Pacific
listen

STARBUCK: (*Looking over the side*) Loveliness unfathomable — as ever lover saw in his young bride's eye. Tell me not of thy teeth-tiered sharks and thy kidnapping cannibal ways — let faith oust fact — let fancy oust memory — I look deep down and do believe.

ISHMAEL AND CREW: A key turns in the lock of the sea-bed
and islands disappear
ships disappear
men disappear
their hearts burst open, the sea flows in
and hulks go drifting through the latitudes
crewed by sailors asleep
the sea looks out of their eyes
it floods the ends of their fingers

like tentacles
like drowned men drifting
the sea turns in on itself

and everything empties into it
islands
ships
sailors

all are the sea's green dream

as lovely as
as lovely as
as lovely as
death

but softer

softer than the death I dream
on my woman's breast

lay down
I dream of you: absence

lay down
I dream of you: absence

lay down
I dream of you: absence

lay down your head
absence

lay down your head
absence

lay down

lay down your head

lay down

(*They are falling asleep.*
From far off, the faint sound of music, dancing, the joyful shouts of men and women.
It draws nearer.
THE CREW *gradually wake up and look across as another ship comes into view.*
AHAB *comes up on deck*)

VOICE, OFF: Come aboard, come aboard.
AHAB: Hast seen the White Whale?
VOICE: No — only heard of him — and don't believe in him, either. But come aboard! We'll soon take that black from your brow. Aye, merry's the play — we're full, and homeward bound.
AHAB: (*To himself*) How wondrous familiar is a fool! (*Aloud*) Well I'm outward bound, and empty. So go thy ways, and I will mine. (*To* **THE CREW**) Forward there! Set all sail, and keep her to the wind!

(**THE CREW** *gradually come to life and go about their business. They cast envious glances at the other ship as the sound slowly fades away*)

FOURTEEN : THE WHALE-WATCH

(*The sea, sunset*)

ISHMAEL: Often it happens in this life — that when fortune's favourites sail close by us, we catch something of their rushing breeze, and feel our own sails fill out. So it seemed with the Pequod. For the day after meeting that homeward craft, whales were seen and four were slain; and one of them by Ahab.

(*The light begins fading down*)

It was well down the afternoon. The four whales had died far from the ship, and wide apart: three of them were brought alongside by nightfall, but the fourth one could not be reached till morning, and the boat that had killed it lay by its side all night, and that boat was Ahab's.

(*It is now night. The whale-boat is moored alongside an enormous black shape; a lantern has been hoisted. In the boat, asleep, are* **QUEEQUEG, DUNDEE, MANXMAN,** *and* **AHAB**; *sitting up, awake, is* **TAHITI**)

Ahab and all his crew were asleep — except for Tahiti, who sat watching as the sharks played around the whale and tapped against the planks of the boat with their tails. Then Ahab started from his slumber and saw Tahiti, face to face. Hooped round by the gloom of the night, they seemed the last men in a flooded world.
AHAB: I have dreamt it again.
TAHITI: Of the hearses? Have I not said, old man, that neither hearse nor coffin can be thine?

AHAB: But none are hearsed that die on the sea.

TAHITI: But I say, old man, that before thou canst die on this voyage, two hearses must be seen by you on the sea — the first not made by mortal hands, and the wood of the second must be grown in America.

AHAB: A strange sight that, Tahiti — a hearse and its plumes floating over the ocean, with the waves for pall-bearers.

TAHITI: Thou canst not die till it be seen, old man.

AHAB: And of thyself?

TAHITI: When it comes to the last, I shall go before thee as thy pilot.

AHAB: And when thou art gone before — if ever that befall — thou must return, to pilot me? How can that be? Then let me take a pledge — I shall slay Moby Dick, and yet survive.

TAHITI: Take another pledge, old man — that only rope can kill thee.

AHAB: The gallows, ye mean. I am immortal then, on land and sea. Immortal on land and sea!

(*Pause*)

ISHMAEL: Both were silent, as one man. The grey dawn came on, the slumbering crew arose from the boat's bottom, and before noon the dead whale was brought to the ship.

FIFTEEN : THE CANDLES

(*Noon. A brilliant day.*
On deck, **AHAB** *and* **SHIP'S COMPANY**.
AHAB *takes a bearing with the quadrant, then steps back to look at the sun*)

AHAB: Thou sea-mark sun! Thou high and mighty pilot! Thou tellest me truly where I *am* — but canst thou cast the least hint where I shall be? Where is Moby Dick? This very instant thou must be eyeing him. (*Looking at the quadrant*) Foolish toy! The world brags of thy cunning, but thou canst not tell where one drop of water will be tomorrow noon — aye, thou insultest the sun with thy impotence! (*Dashing it to the deck*) No more will I follow thee. The ship's compass, and that only, shall point my way on the sea. (*To* **THE HELMSMAN**) Turn her prow to the Line, make east-south-east her course. (*Shouts to* **THE CREW**) East-south-east for the White Whale!

THE CREW: East-south-east for the White Whale! East-south-east for Moby Dick!

(*They sing snatches of 'The Whaling Song' as they go about their work.*
AHAB *returns to his cabin to look at the chart*)

STARBUCK: (*Watching him go*) I have sat before a coal fire and watched it all aglow, full of tormented, flaming life — and I have seen it wane down at last, down to dumbest dust. Old man of oceans! Of all this fiery life of thine, what shall at last remain but one little heap of ashes!

STUBB: Aye, but sea-coal ashes — mind ye that, Mr. Starbuck, sea-coal, not your common coal. Well, well — I heard Ahab mutter "Someone thrusts these cards into my hands, and swears that I must play them, and no others". (*Looking towards* AHAB'S *cabin*) And damn me, Ahab, but thou actest right — live in the game, and die in it!

(*There is a sudden tremendous clap of thunder. The sky darkens, the wind rises, and rain begins to fall in torrents. The ship rocks from side to side, waves break over the deck.* STARBUCK *and* STUBB *yell instructions as* THE CREW *rush hither and thither, securing ropes etc.*
Darkness falls, and then a flash of lightning strikes the mast where the doubloon is nailed.
STUBB *begins to sing*)

STARBUCK: Avast, Stubb! Let the typhoon sing and strike his harp in our rigging, but if thou art a brave man thou wilt hold thy peace.
STUBB: But I am not a brave man. I am a coward, and I sing to keep up my spirits. And I tell you, Mr. Starbuck, there's no way to stop me singing but to cut my throat. (*Starts to sing again*)
STARBUCK: Fool! Look through my eyes if thou hast none of thine own.
STUBB: What? Canst thou see better of a dark night than anyone else, no matter how foolish?
STARBUCK: Here! (*Seizing* STUBB *by the shoulder*) Markest thou not that the gale comes from the east, the very course that Ahab runs for Moby Dick? The very course he swung to this day noon? Seest thou not where the lightning struck? At the very mast where he nailed the doubloon, man! Now jump overboard, and sing away if thou must!
STUBB: I don't understand ye — what's in the wind?
STARBUCK: (*Ignoring him*) Aye — back round the Cape is the shortest way to Nantucket — and this gale that hammers against us could yet be the fair wind that drives us home. Yonder is all blackness and doom — but there, to leeward — (*with a start*)— who's there?
AHAB: (*Groping his way along the deck*) Old Thunder!

(*There is another sudden flash. The three mastheads burst into white flame, giving the effect of three burning crosses*)

STUBB: (*Pointing*) Look aloft! The corpusants! (*Kneeling on the deck*) The corpusants have mercy on us all!

(THE CREW *are gathered together on the deck, all staring upwards*)

STARBUCK: (*To* STUBB) What thinkest thou now? Is't time for a song?

(*The flames die down*)

STUBB: No, it isn't. I said the corpusants have mercy on us, and I hope they will. But do they only have mercy on long faces? Have they no bowels for a laugh? And hear me, Mr. Starbuck — I take these masthead flames for a sign of good luck — for those masts are rooted in a hold that is going to be chock-full of sperm-oil, d'ye see, and all that sperm will work up into the masts, like sap in a tree.

(*The three mastheads again burst into flame*)

The corpusants have mercy on us all!
AHAB: Aye men, look up at it — and mark it well, for the white flame lights the way to the White Whale! (*Brandishing a harpoon, he shouts up at the flames*) Oh thou clear spirit of clear fire, I now know that thy right worship is defiance. To neither love nor reverence wilt thou be kind. No fearless fool now fronts thee. (*With a sweep of his arm*) In the midst of all things impersonal, to the last gasp of my earth-quake life, a personality stands here. Oh thou clear spirit, of thy fire thou madest me, and like a true child of fire I breathe it back to thee.

(*He throws down the harpoon.*
Sudden, repeated flashes of lightning — the flames leap up in height)

Thou canst blind, but I can then grope. Thou canst consume, but I can then be ashes. The lightning burns my skull, my eyeballs ache, my brain is plucked and rolling on the ground. But yet I'll speak to thee, thou light leaping out of darkness. And I am darkness leaping out of light, leaping out of thee! There burn the flames. I glory in my birthright — thou art my fiery father, my sweet mother I know not. Leap! Leap up, and lick the sky! I leap with thee, I burn with thee — oh spirit of fire, let me be welded to thee!

(*A flash of lightning strikes* **AHAB'S** *harpoon, which bursts into flames*)

STARBUCK: The lance! Look at thy lance, old man! (*Grasping* **AHAB** *by the arm*) God, *God* is against thee, old man — forbear! 'Tis an ill voyage — let us square the yards, and look for a fair wind homeward.

(*Shouting agreement,* **THE CREW** *run to catch hold of the ropes*)

AHAB: (*Brandishing the burning harpoon*) Touch not a rope's end — do, and I'll transfix ye!

(*The frightened* **CREW** *fall back*)

All your oaths to hunt the White Whale are as binding as mine. And heart, and soul, and body, and lungs, and life, Ahab is bound — and so are ye. His heart pounds to that beat and no other — and look ye, see how I blow out the last fear!

(*He blows out the flame on the harpoon.*
THE CREW *and* **STUBB** *run from the deck, leaving* **AHAB, STARBUCK,** *and* **TAHITI**)

SIXTEEN : THE MUSKET

(The deck, later that night.
The typhoon has abated. Still the sound of wind.
TAHITI *is at the helm; standing beside him,* **STARBUCK**. *Below,* **AHAB** *is*
asleep in his cabin, a lighted lantern swinging above his head)

STARBUCK: (*To* **TAHITI**) Can you steer the course?
TAHITI: The course?
STARBUCK: Now that the wind's come round astern.

(*Pause*)

TAHITI: East-south-east it is, sir.
STARBUCK: I'll tell the Captain.

(*He goes below, discovers* **AHAB** *asleep in the cabin)*

He would have shot me once. Aye, and there's the very musket he pointed at me.
(*He slowly picks up the musket*) Loaded. That's not good. But wait — I'll cure myself
of this. I came to report a fair wind to him. But how fair? Fair for death and doom,
and fair for Moby Dick — it's a fair wind that's only fair for that accursed fish. The
very tube he pointed at me — he would have killed me with the very thing I han-
dle now. Aye, and kill the whole crew with me. Has he not dashed his heavenly
quadrant? But shall this crazed old man be allowed to drag a whole ship's company to doom with him? Aye, it would make him the wilful murderer of us all, if
this ship came to harm — and come to harm it will, if Ahab have his way. If then,
he were this instant — *put aside* — that crime would not be his.

(*He points the musket towards the sleeping* **AHAB**, *then lowers it)*

[Great God forbid! Is there no other way? No lawful way? Make him a prisoner to
be taken home? What! Hope to wrest this old man's power from his living hands?
Only a fool would try it. Say he were pinioned even — knotted all over with ropes
and hawsers, chained down to ring-bolts on this cabin floor — he would be more
hideous than a caged beast. I could not endure the sight. What then remains?] I
stand here upon an open sea, with two oceans between me and law. Is heaven a
murderer when its lightning strikes a murderer in his bed? And would I be a murderer if —

(*He slowly raises the musket again)*

A touch, a gentle touch, and Starbuck may survive to hug his wife and child again.
Oh Mary, Mary! Boy, boy, boy! If I wake thee not to death, old man, then who can
tell to what unsounded depths Starbuck may sink, with all the crew. Great God,
where art thou? Shall I? Shall I?

(*A long pause. He slowly lowers the musket, then speaks quietly*)

The wind has eased and shifted, sir. She heads her course.
AHAB: (*In his sleep*) Stern all! Oh Moby Dick, I clutch thy heart at last!

(**STARBUCK** *hesitates a moment longer, then returns the musket to the rack and leaves the cabin*)

SEVENTEEN : THE LIFE-BUOY

(*Morning.*
AHAB, STUBB, *and* **THE CREW** *on deck*
A high-pitched, crying sound is heard, some way off. **THE CREW** *are uneasy*)

DUNDEE: Mermaids.
PIP: 'Tis Pip, who jumped from the whale-boat. Hey, Pip!
STUBB: Avast! 'Tis —
MANXMAN: 'Tis the sound of men new-drowned in the sea.

(*Pause/the sound is heard again*)

'Tis the sound of their souls, crying to be let into heaven.
DUNDEE: Is it not mermaids?
MANXMAN: 'Tis drowned men, I tell ye.
AHAB: (*To* **MANXMAN**) Where wast thou born?
MANXMAN: On the rocky little Isle of Man, sir.
AHAB: A man from Man — and wouldst thou unman my crew by talk of men new-drowned? Hast thou never heard — of seals?

(**STARBUCK** *comes up on deck*)

Mr. Starbuck — what damage done in the storm?
STARBUCK: Nothing of note, sir, save —
AHAB: Save what, man?
STARBUCK: Save the life-buoy, sir — 'tis gone to the bottom.
AHAB: Then let the carpenter make another life-buoy — see to it, Mr. Starbuck.
MANXMAN: (*Picking up the line*) All's work in a wicked world. (**PIP** *approaches*) Come to help, eh Pip?
PIP: Pip? Whom call ye Pip? Pip jumped from the whale-boat. Pip's missing. Let's see if ye haven't fished him up here, fisherman. It drags hard, he must be holding on. Jerk him, Queequeg! Throw him off, we haul in no cowards here. Ho — here's his arm breaking water. A hachet! A hachet to cut it off with! Captain Ahab, sir! Here's Pip, trying to get on board again.
MANXMAN: Peace, thou crazy loon. (*Pushing* **PIP**) Away from the quarterdeck!
AHAB: (*To* **MANXMAN**) Hands off that holiness! (*To* **PIP**) Where sayest thou Pip was, boy?

PIP: Astern there, sir. There, lo!

AHAB: And who art thou, boy? I see not my reflection in thy eyes. Who art thou?

PIP: Bell-boy, sir. Ding, dong, ding! Pip! Pip! One hundred pounds of clay reward for Pip — six feet high, but cowardly — best known by that. Ding, dong, ding! Who's seen Pip the coward?

AHAB: Oh ye heavens, look down here. Ye did beget this luckless child, and have abandoned him. Here. (*Taking* **PIP'S** *hand*) Thou touchest my inmost centre, boy. Ahab's cabin shall be Pip's home.

PIP: (*Feeling* **AHAB'S** *hand*) Here's velvet shark-skin. Had poor Pip felt such a thing as this, perhaps he'd ne'er been lost. This is a man-rope, something that weak souls may cling to. Let Manxman come and rivet these two hands together, for I will not let this go.

AHAB: No, nor will I boy — come, to my cabin.

(**AHAB** *and* **PIP** *go off*)

MANXMAN: There go two daft ones — the one daft with strength, and the other daft with weakness. But make a new life-buoy? Well, all's work in a wicked world. (*Starts to gather his tools together*)

(**QUEEQUEG** *comes up to him*)

QUEEQUEG: (*Pointing to the coffin*) Use Queequeg's canoe.

MANXMAN: Canoe? You mean — Mr. Starbuck! Queequeg says I'm to use his coffin for a life-buoy. Shall I —

STARBUCK: A life-buoy of a coffin?

STUBB: Rather queer that, I should say.

(*Pause*)

STARBUCK: Rig it, carpenter. The coffin, I mean. Do not look at me so — dost thou hear me? Rig it.

MANXMAN: And shall I nail down the lid, sir?

STARBUCK: Aye.

MANXMAN: And shall I then caulk the seams, sir?

STARBUCK: Aye.

MANXMAN: And shall I then go over it with pitch, sir?

STARBUCK: Away! What possesses thee to this? Make a life-buoy of the coffin, and no more. Come, Mr. Stubb.

(**STARBUCK** *and* **STUBB** *go off*)

MANXMAN: (*Looking at the coffin*) I don't like this, it's a cobbling job. Let tinkers' brats do the cobbling, a carpenter's for better things. I like to take in hand none but clean, virgin, fair and square mathematical jobs, something that begins regularly at the beginning, and is at the middle when midway, and comes to an end at the conclusion — not a cobbler's job that's at an end in the middle. It's an old woman's trick to be giving cobbling jobs. Lord — what an affection old women have for tinkers. I knew an old woman of sixty-five who ran away with a bald-headed young tinker once. And that's the reason I would never work for lonely old widow-women ashore — they might have taken it into their heads to run off with me. And then where would I have been? Not out here in the middle of the ocean, that's for certain.

(*He begins work on the coffin.* **QUEEQUEG** *sits down to watch him*)

MANXMAN: (*Sings as he works*)

Oh the whales they are full size where we sail,
        where we sail
oh the whales they are full size, where we sail
oh the whales they are full size
but we'll stab them through their eyes
as we hunt them for our prize, where we sail
        where we sail

Oh I wish we were like geese flying west,
        flying west
oh I wish we were like geese, flying west
oh I wish we were like geese
for we'd live and die in peace
till the hour of our decease, in our nests
        in our nests

Oh we're out upon the waves where we sail,
        where we sail
oh we're out upon the waves, where we sail
oh we're out upon the waves
hoping God who loves and saves
will yet bring us to safe graves, where we sail
        where we sail

(**AHAB** *comes back on deck*)

AHAB: What's here?
MANXMAN: Life-buoy, sir. Mr. Starbuck's orders.
AHAB: Art thou not an arrant, inter-meddling, heathenish scamp to be one day making coffins, and the next to be making life-buoys out of these same coffins, and then to sing coffin songs whilst making of these same life-buoys? Thou art as un-principled as the gods, or a gravedigger.
MANXMAN: Faith, sir —
AHAB: Faith? What's that?
MANXMAN: Why sir, it's a sort of exclamation, like —
AHAB: Art thou a silkworm? Dost thou spin thy own shroud out of thyself? Dispatch! (*Goes a little way off*)

(**MANXMAN** *hammers on the coffin*
AHAB *listens impatiently for a few moments, then turns suddenly*)

AHAB: Will ye never have done, carpenter, with that accursed sound? (*Goes*)

(**MANXMAN** *watches as he goes, then hammers harder on the coffin*)

EIGHTEEN : THE PEQUOD MEETS THE RACHEL

(**AHAB** *and* **SHIP'S COMPANY** *on deck*)

STUBB: (*Peering over the side*) Ship Rachel, out of Nantucket. In a hurry.
AHAB: (*Shouting*) Hast seen the White Whale?
VOICE, OFF: Aye, yesterday. Have ye seen a whale-boat adrift?
STARBUCK: (*To* **THE CREW**) Help him aboard.

(**CAPTAIN GARDINER** *of the 'Rachel' clambers over the side*)

AHAB: (*Going up to him*) Where was he? Not killed?
GARDINER: (*Holds onto the rail, pauses before he speaks*)
    Late in the afternoon. Of yesterday.
    To windward, four miles off. We saw
    a shoal of whales. Lowered three boats.
    And then, to leeward, saw the head and hump
    of Moby Dick. Lowered again —
    a fourth boat, our reserve. Watched as she chased,
    then fastened him — at which he threw on speed
    and soon gained the horizon, towing our boat behind.

    We followed in the ship, but first were forced
    to make a windward sweep, pick up
    the other three. The night came on.
    We struck our former course, but of the missing boat
    found not a sign.

AHAB: And of the whale?
GARDINER: And of the whale, or of the missing boat,
    found not a sign.
    Since then we've searched for eighteen hours,
    crowded the masts, lit beacons on the deck
    … in vain.

        But if you joined our search —

(*He looks imploringly at* **AHAB.** *The two of them turn aside in private conversation*)

STUBB: I'll wager that someone in that missing boat wore the Captain's best coat, or maybe his watch — whoever heard of two pious whale-ships cruising after one missing boat in the height of the whaling season? See how pale he looks, pale in the very buttons of his eyes — it can't have been a coat, it must have been —
GARDINER: (*To* **AHAB**) My boy, *my own boy* is among them. For God's sake — for eight and forty hours let me charter your ship. I will gladly pay for it, and roundly pay for it, if there be no other way. For eight and forty hours only — you must, oh you must, you *shall* do this thing.
STUBB: His son! It's his son he's lost! I take back the watch and coat. We must save that boy.
MANXMAN: (*Quietly*) He's drowned with the rest of them, last night. We heard their spirits. *Ye* sail upon his tomb.

(*Pause/all freeze except* **GARDINER** *and* **AHAB**)

GARDINER: I will not go until you say *aye* to me. For you too have a boy, Captain Ahab — though but a child, and nestling safe at home now — a child of your old age. Yes, you relent — I see it. (*To* **THE CREW**) Run, run, men, and stand by to square in the yards.

(*No-one moves*)

AHAB: (*Slowly*) Captain Gardiner, I will not do it. Even now I lose time. God bless ye man, and may I forgive myself, but I must go. (*Turning away*) Mr. Starbuck, look at the binnacle watch, and in three minutes from this present instant warn off all strangers — then brace forward, and let the ship sail as before.

(*He turns abruptly and goes below to his cabin.*
GARDINER *stands staring after him. Then, as if starting from a dream, he turns and hurries to the side, disappears.*
THE CREW *unfreeze and go about their tasks, like statues slowly coming to life*)

NINETEEN : AHAB AND PIP IN THE CABIN

(**AHAB** *and* **PIP** *in the cabin.*
AHAB *stands to leave,* **PIP** *catches him by the hand*)

AHAB: No lad, thou must not follow Ahab now. There is that in thee which I feel too curing to my malady. Like cures like — and for this hunt my malady becomes my most desired health. Stay here, where they shall serve thee as the Captain. Aye lad, sit here in my own screwed chair — another screw to it, thou shalt be.
PIP: No, no, no! Ye have not a whole body, sir — then use me as your own lost leg, and find your way with me.

(*He kneels, holds* **AHAB** *by the leg*)

They say that Stubb did once desert poor Pip — whose drowned bones now show white, for all the blackness of his living skin. But I will never desert you, sir, as Stubb did him.

AHAB: When thou speakest thus, then Ahab's purpose keels up in him — I tell thee no, it cannot be.

PIP: Oh good master, master, master!

AHAB: (*Breaking away*) Weep so, and I will murder thee! (*Then, softer*) Listen, and thou wilt hear my ivory foot upon the deck, and know that I am there. Thy hand — met! True art thou, lad, as the circumference to its centre. God forever bless thee — and, if it come to that, God forever save thee, let what will befall.

(*He goes on deck*)

PIP: Here he this instant stood. I stand in his air — but I'm alone. If poor Pip were here I could endure it, but he's missing. Ding, dong, ding! Pip! Pip! Who's seen Pip? He must be up here. Let's try the door. What? Neither lock nor bolt, yet there's no opening it. It must be the spell. He said to stay here, aye, and told me this screwed chair was mine. I'll sit here as an admiral, and lord it over rows of captains and lieutenants. Ha! What's this? Epaulettes! The epaulettes come crowding! Pass round the decanters. Glad to see ye — fill up, monsieurs! What a strange feeling, now, when a black boy's host to white men with gold braid upon their coats! Monsieurs, have ye seen one Pip? Negro lad, six feet high, but cowardly. Jumped from a whale-boat once — seen him? No? Well then, fill up again, captains, and let's drink shame upon all cowards! I name no names. Shame upon them! Put one foot upon the table. Shame upon all cowards. Hist! Above there, I hear ivory — oh master, master! I am indeed downhearted, when you walk over me. But here I'll stay, though this stern strike rocks, and oysters come to join me.

TWENTY : THE CHASE

(*A clear, steel-blue day.*
SHIP'S COMPANY *on deck. To one side, looking out to sea,* **AHAB** *and* **STARBUCK**. *On the other side of* **AHAB**, *standing a little way off, is* **TAHITI**)

STARBUCK:

When I come home
from the sky and the ocean
I will open the door
and the sky and the ocean
will fill up the house
in the way that silence
might fill a cathedral.

(*Pause*)

When I come home.

AHAB: Starbuck!

(**STARBUCK** *turns to him*)

It is a mild, mild wind, and a mild-looking sky, Starbuck. On such a day I struck my first whale — forty, forty years ago. (*Suddenly*) What a fool, what a forty years fool, has old Ahab been! Forty years of continual whaling, the blood of a thousand lowerings — and yet how much wiser or richer is Ahab now? Do I not look old, so very, very old, Starbuck?

(*Pause*)

Come closer, Starbuck, let me look into a human eye.

(**STARBUCK** *moves closer,* **AHAB** *stares into his eyes*)

But this is the magic glass — I see my wife and child in thine eye. Thou shalt not lower when Ahab gives chase to Moby Dick, that risk shall not be thine — not with the far-away home I see in thine eye!
STARBUCK: (*Grasping* **AHAB'S** *hand*) But why should anyone give chase to that hateful fish! Away, and let us home! I think, sir, they have mild blue days, even as this, in Nantucket.
AHAB: They have — and I have seen them, some summer days in the morning. About this time the boy wakes, sits up in bed — and his mother tells him of how I am abroad on the deep, but will yet come home to dance with him again.
STARBUCK: 'Tis my Mary, my Mary herself! She promised that my boy, every morning, should be carried to the hill to catch the first glimpse of his father's sail! Come Captain, study the course and let us away — see the boy's face from the window, the boy's hand on the hill!
AHAB: (*Stares at him, then turns to look out to sea*) What is it that commands me, that I must keep pushing, and crowding, and jamming myself all the time — and doing what in my proper, natural state I'd never dare? Is Ahab, Ahab? Is it I, God, or who that lifts this arm? If the sun and stars revolve but by some hidden power, then how can this heart beat, this one small brain think thoughts, unless God does that beating, that thinking, that *living*, and not I? By heaven, man, we are turned around in this world like yonder windlass, and Fate is the handspike. And if God does this (*raises his arm*), then is not God turned round with us? Who's to doom, when the judge himself is dragged to the bar?

(*A pause, he turns*)

Eh, Starbuck?

(*But* **STARBUCK** *has moved away*)

AHAB: (*Staring out to sea*) Behind closed doors, trapped forever. There is only one place for a man to live, and that is under the sky.
TAHITI: And to die also, Captain?

(**AHAB** *turns to look at him*)

Are indoor deaths just for women?

(*Pause*)

AHAB: D'ye hold to your prophecy?
TAHITI: (*Doesn't answer*)
AHAB: Then do, and I'll to mine. (*Shouts aloft*) What d'ye see?
LOOK-OUT: Nothing, sir.
AHAB: No sign? Are ye sure? (*To* **THE CREW**) Hoist me aloft.

(*They do so, using a rope basket. Halfway up the mast* **AHAB** *lets out a wild shout*)

There she blows, there she blows! A hump like a snow-hill — it is Moby Dick!

(*Pandemonium on deck as* **AHAB** *is lowered down*)

And did none of ye see him before?
MANXMAN: I saw him almost the same instant, sir, that Captain Ahab did, and I cried out.
AHAB: But not the *same* instant, not the *same* instant. No, the doubloon is mine — fate reserved it for me — none of ye could have raised him. There she blows! There she blows! There she blows! Again! Stand by to lower, Mr. Stubb. Look to the ship, Mr. Starbuck.

(**STARBUCK** *remains on deck whilst* **AHAB, QUEEQUEG, ISHMAEL, DUNDEE,** *and* **TAHITI** *are lowered in the boat*)

ISHMAEL: Imagine this:
          a sky of perfect blue
and under it, stretched like a sheet of glass,
the sea
        — so blue, you'd need brown eyes
to notice it.
Direct ahead, breaking this symmetry,
a massive blob of white
              — as if some god,
flying above Antarctica, had plucked an iceberg up
and dropped it here, half-way across the world.
Above it hover flocks of screaming gulls.
Whilst there — embedded in its snowy peak
your eyes make out:
              what seems to be a spear.
(As if upon this pure white beach
some child had left a spade).

The iceberg disappears.
From where it sank the small waves widen out
like ripples on a pond.
The gulls fly off.
And nothing's left to mark the spot
except:
        a small black speck, with men in it.
This is the boat.
Some distance off, a larger speck: the ship.
They wait.
They wait an hour.

And then:

QUEEQUEG: The birds! The birds!
ISHMAEL: A bird's eyesight is keener than a man's
        and these have seen:
                    the iceberg, coming up.
        And then

IT SURFACES.

Faster than light
the two harpoons are thrown.
The two lines hold.
And yet.

The world was blue.
It now turns white
and, in an instant, black:
as if a marble tomb had opened up
showing the grave beneath.

It is his mouth, the mouth of Moby Dick.

And inside it, two rows of gravestone teeth
which slice clean through the boat.

Men cling to either end — two here,
one here,
and here another one
— how many men is that?
And all this time the whale is circling
and ploughing a groove in the sea,
and Ahab — he is one of them —
and Ahab shouts:
[AHAB: (*In the water*) Sail on the —
ISHMAEL: And then his words are lost,

drowned in the spray
churned up by Moby Dick.
Again:]
AHAB: Sail on the whale! Sail on the whale and drive him off!
ISHMAEL: And then the whale turns,
a little sulkily, as the black prow
bears down on him,
and swims a little way off,
and watches idly
as from the ship they lower a second boat,
and having seen all this — is gone.
AHAB: (*Climbing aboard, soaked through*) Are the men safe? Where is — (*With a sudden roar of anguish*) — Tahiti! Run — run, all of ye — above, below, cabin, forecastle, find him!
ISHMAEL: But no one moves.
DUNDEE: I saw him caught by the line, sir — when the whale struck.
AHAB: And then?
ISHMAEL: But no one answers.
AHAB: (*Turning aside*) Thou was to go before, but still be seen before I perish — how's that, Tahiti? Wouldst not answer then, and canst not now. (*He turns back to them*) Where is the whale?
STARBUCK: Two miles to leeward, sir, and swimming strongly.
AHAB: Then pile on sail, and follow that same course. (*Advancing towards the doubloon*) Men, this gold is mine, for I earned it — but here let it stay till the White Whale is killed. And whosoever of ye first raises him on that day, he shall have the doubloon — and if on that day I again shall raise him, then ten times its sum shall be divided amongst ye.

(**THE CREW** *cheer*)

AHAB: (*To* **STARBUCK**) The deck is thine, sir. (*Goes below*)
ISHMAEL: And night came on, and that was the end of the first day.

(*Lighting change*)

ISHMAEL: Sometimes,
far out at sea,
ahead of you, you'll sight a rock,
and at that instant, suddenly,
you want to hold your course, head into it
— for nothing more
than pure delight in recklessness;
to hear the dreadful sound of keel on rock,
and water rushing in.
And in those seconds whilst the ship ploughs on
towards oblivion, you are as young
as you will ever be.
Until with heavy hands you alter course

and come back to your life.

So now:
all through that second day
the ship tore on,
leaving a furrow in the sea.
The rigging lived:
like trees laden with fruit
the mastheads crawled with men,
all straining for a glimpse
of that one thing
which might destroy them all.
Ahead, destuction lay, and yet
all through that second day
the shouts and counter-shouts rang out for him
as if the whale were Christmas, and safe home;
whilst back and forth across the deck
Ahab forever paced, and turned
— a hundred times that day he turned —
to shout:

AHAB: Aloft there! Which way now?

LOOK-OUT: Still two miles off, and dead to leeward, sir.

AHAB: (*To himself*) He lures me on — to what? (*To* **STARBUCK**) More sail!

ISHMAEL: Again.

AHAB: Aloft there! Which way now?

LOOK-OUT: Still dead to leeward, sir.

ISHMAEL: And yet again.

AHAB: Aloft there! Which way now?

LOOK-OUT: No change — still dead to leeward, sir.

AHAB: (*To* **STARBUCK**) More sail — more sail, I say!

(*The lights begin fading down*)

STARBUCK: (*To the heavens*) Great God! But for one instant show thyself! (*To* **AHAB**) Never, never wilt thou capture him, old man. Two days chased, thy boat stove to splinters, a man lost, a host of good angels mobbing thee with warnings — what more wouldst thou have? Shall we keep chasing this murderous fish till he swamp the last man? Shall we be towed by him to the infernal world?

AHAB: Ahab is forever Ahab, man. This whole act's immutably decreed — 'twas rehearsed by thee and me a billion years before this ocean rolled. Fool! I am the Fates' lieutenant — I act under orders. Look that thou obeyest mine. (*To* **THE CREW**) Believe ye in the things called omens? Then laugh — for ere they sink, drowning things will rise twice to the surface — then rise again, to sink for evermore. And so with Moby Dick — two days he's floated, tomorrow will be the third. Aye men, he'll rise once more — but only to spout his last! D'ye feel brave, men, brave?

(**THE CREW** *cheer.* **STARBUCK** *has turned away*)

LOOK-OUT: Can't see the spout now, sir — too dark.
AHAB: How heading when last seen?
LOOK-OUT: As before, sir — straight to leeward.
AHAB: Good — he will travel slower now 'tis night. Down royals and top-gallant sails, Mr. Starbuck — we must not run over him before morning. (*Goes below*)
ISHMAEL: And that was the end of the second day.

(*Lighting change*)

AHAB: D'ye see him?
LOOK-OUT: Nothing yet, sir.
AHAB: But in his wake though — must be, must be. Here's another day like the beginning of the world — a bright new world, made for angels to play in. There's food for thought, eh Starbuck? But Ahab never thinks, he only feels — that's tingling enough for mortal man. To think's audacity — only God has that privilege. Aloft there! What d'ye see?
LOOK-OUT: Nothing, sir.
AHAB: Nothing! And noon at hand — the doubloon goes a-begging! But wait — I should have sighted him by now — I've sailed over him — but how, and him with a two mile start? Fool — the lines! The harpoons he's towing, they've slowed him down at last. (*Shouts*) About! About! Bring her to windward!
STARBUCK: Aye, aye, sir. (*To himself*) Against the wind he steers for the open jaw. God keep us, for already my bones feel damp within me, and from the inside wet my flesh. Oh God — I fear I disobey thee in obeying him!
ISHMAEL: An hour goes by. And then.

AHAB: (*Suddenly shouts, and immediately his shout is taken up by the whole* **CREW**) There she blows! 'Tis him, 'tis him — 'tis Moby Dick! Prepare to lower, Mr.Stubb.

(*Preparations are made for the lowering*)

AHAB: Starbuck!
STARBUCK: Sir?
AHAB: 'Tis the third day, Starbuck — again I go to meet him.
STARBUCK: Aye, sir — for thou wilt have it so.

(*Pause*)

AHAB: I am old, Starbuck — shake hands with me, man.
STARBUCK: (*In tears, shaking* **AHAB'S** *hand*) I beg thee, sir — see, 'tis a brave man that weeps — I beg —
AHAB: (*Turning away from him*) Lower away!

(*The boat is lowered into the water —* **QUEEQUEG, ISHMAEL, MANXMAN,** *and* **DUNDEE** *are the oarsmen, with* **AHAB** *at the helm.* **STARBUCK** *remains on deck*)

Pull for the whale!
STARBUCK: (*Alone on deck*) When three days flow together in one pursuit, be sure

that the first is morning, the second noon, and the third — evening, and the end of the thing. My God — what is this that shoots through me, and leaves me so deadly calm, and yet expectant — fixed at the top of a shudder! Masthead there! D'ye see my boy's hand on the hill? Crazed — stir thyself, Starbuck. Masthead — keep thy keenest eye on the boat! Mark well the whale!

(*On the sea:*)

ISHMAEL: The whale has dived.
>   And as before, they wait
>   — knowing he will, he must, come up.

>   And so they wait.

>   And death hangs
>   under the sea
>   like a white bell
>   in a tall tower.

DUNDEE: (*To himself*) It is here again, now. But this time I won't forget it.

(**MANXMAN** *makes the sign of the cross over the water*)

ISHMAEL: What —
MANXMAN: For him — Tahiti. Wherever he is.
QUEEQUEG: All dead men go to the stars.
ISHMAEL: Even if they die at sea?
QUEEQUEG: Especially then — for all seaways lead to the stars.
DUNDEE: (*Still to himself*) I won't forget it. I know I won't.
AHAB: (*Suddenly shouting back to the ship*) Drive off that hawk from the masthead! He pecks at the flag!
ISHMAEL: And like a stone
>   dropped in a quiet pond
>   his shout comes back to them
>   and breaks the spell.

>   (**MOBY DICK** *rises out of the water.*
>   *The boat rocks violently.*
>   **AHAB** *stands, ready to throw his harpoon.*
>   **MOBY DICK** *turns sideways on — and there, lashed to his flank by whale-lines, is*
>   *the half-torn body of* **TAHITI**)

AHAB: (*Dropping his harpoon*) Fooled — fooled — fooled! I do see thee again — and this is the hearse thou didst promise.
ISHMAEL: The whale swims off, towards the open sea.
AHAB: Pull on — and after him!
ISHMAEL: Now Ahab stands with his harpoon
>   and feels his hatred in his hand,
>   and waits.

And the whale turns, and seems to wait.

And in a house eight thousand miles away
a woman grips a chair,
and feels: her widowhood.

And then the thing is thrown.

It strikes.
The line goes tight.
But then the whale jerks back his head
— just as a man might brush a fly —
and SNAPS it through
which jolts the boat
and throws someone —
DUNDEE: Man overboard! He's —
AHAB: Gone.
ISHMAEL: The whale swims off.
AHAB: Pull on — and after him! Now, whale —
ISHMAEL: Now: whale.

And now, and now,
and ever now,
is: whale.

For something stirs in him: perhaps
it is the tip of Ahab's lance
that conjures this, or else some dream
he'd buried fathoms deep inside himself
now surfaces, and says:

NOW:

WHALE.

THE CREW: The ship! He heads for the ship!
STARBUCK: (*On deck*) Up helm — he comes this way! All ye sweet powers of air,
now hug me close. Up helm, I say! Too late! Oh Ahab, this is thy work! My God,
stand by me now!

(*There is a tremendous crash as the whale strikes the ship*)

AHAB: My ship! The hearse, the second hearse!

ISHMAEL AND CREW:	And the seas come spilling over	
	and the deck	disappears
	and the three tall masts	disappear
	and the black flag at the masthead	disappears
	and the ocean opens	

like a huge mouth
whilst above, the wild birds fly
and the sea closes over,
like a shroud.

AHAB: Death-glorious ship! Must ye then perish, and without me? (*He picks up a harpoon*) I am drawn to thee yet, thou all-destroying whale. To the last I grapple with thee; from hell's heart I stab at thee; for hate's sake I spit my last breath at thee. Sink all coffins and hearses to one common pool! And since neither can be mine, let me be towed forever, still tied to thee, thou accursed whale!

(*He hurls the harpoon*)

DUNDEE/MANXMAN/QUEEQUEG: (*Each speaking a line in turn*)
Through a groove in the air
the iron is darted
the whale is struck
but the line runs foul
and now a dead man
stoops to clear it

(*As **AHAB** bends over, the line frees itself and catches him around the neck, throwing him into the water*)

ISHMAEL: and is gone.

And the whale rolls over slowly
and brings his great head against the boat
— as when the autumn wind,
having nothing better to do,
scatters dead leaves
and tosses them idly
into a ditch.

And all are gone.

Save one.

(*Lighting change.
The life-buoy coffin bobs up, with **ISHMAEL** clinging to it*)

Save all.

For when the ship went down
not only I
survived the wreck
but all in space and time

who did not drown in her.

And yet:

(*Lights up on* **THE CHORUS OF THE DROWNED**)

CHORUS OF THE DROWNED: Death hangs
under the sea
like a white bell
in a tall tower.

Death sounds
like the note of a bell
over again
the note is repeated.

Death hangs
just under the sea
again and again
the waves are repeated.

Contemporary Theatre Review, 1996,
Vol. 5, 3–4 pp. 153–154
Reprints available directly from the publisher
Photocopying permitted by license only

Each Must Bear A Harpoon

Rod Wooden

(An edited version of this short piece was printed in The Independent *on 21st September 1994. It is published here in full for the first time.)*

Why did you bother? This was the question asked by many of the national critics when my stage version of Herman Melville's *Moby Dick* opened at the RSC's The Other Place in Stratford-upon-Avon last autumn.

Like true theatre, the novel *Moby Dick* is not *about* something, it *is* something: it is not so much the story of Captain Ahab's search for the white whale as the experience of that search. And here lies the difficulty. For we have become used to being told what art is *about*, to having it explained for us – so much so that when we are invited to actually experience something, we are at a loss.

A terrible neatness has been born, a neatness which would reduce theatre to staged journalism. We have become trapped into thinking that if we put as little as possible of life onto the stage, then we may stand a chance of getting it right. But of course there is no 'right' to get to, which is something that Melville supremely recognised when he tried to cram the whole of his life, and all his wildest dreams, onto the page. He was not interested in literal truth, but only in the truth as he saw it, a terrible poetic truth: that human hubris can bring forth savage monsters, which have the power to destroy us all.

Ahab's ego is such that he cannot accept the existence of anything stronger than himself; faced with the terror of a God-less universe, then he, Ahab, must rush to occupy the space that God has vacated. Melville's novel is an epic poem, a Greek tragedy. It cannot be staged using conventional language. What evolved over weeks of rehearsal with the actors and director Gerry Mulgrew was a highly stylised, poetic form, which could be adapted to meet the constantly changing demands of the narrative: thus the story of the mysterious spirit-spout uses conventional iambic pentameters, whilst the final episode of the whale chase employs a much more broken rhythm, to allow for the swirling physical activity which Gerry's staging brings to the scene. Finally, Karen Wimhurst's music was added, sometimes to heighten, at other times to deliberately counter the action.

When we opened last autumn, the mix was not right. The harpoons of the press came flying. Brave but foolhardy, ostentatious, flawed, uneven – these were some of the politer adjectives that were used. There were complaints that the play was not the novel. Most of the reviews seemed to consist of a check list: you have got this right, but this, this and this are wrong. Neatness is all. The general consensus was that we had attempted the impossible, and had failed. We disagreed. We felt that the production was still evolving and that our mistake had been to think we could achieve a polished, finished result in such a short period of time. Twice during the Stratford run we returned to work on it, encouraged by some warm audiences and by the total commitment of the actors. In London over the last three weeks, the work has continued. What is an epic on the page had to become an epic on the stage also. Slowly, steadily, we feel it has done so.

'I myself am a savage', wrote Melville, 'owing no allegiance but to the King of Cannibals, and ready at any moment to rebel against him'. Perhaps we do not have enough savagery in our theatres, which is why we are seeing an increasing savagery on our streets. We need to bring our demons out into the light and stare at them, as Melville did. They may drown us, but if we try to avoid them they will surely drown us anyway. Again, we await the reviews. Stare on.

Contemporary Theatre Review,
1996, Vol. 5, 3–4 pp. 155–157
Reprints available directly from the publisher
Photocopying permitted by license only

© 1996 OPA (Overseas Publishers Association)
Amsterdam B.V. Published in The Netherlands
by Harwood Academic Publishers GmbH
Printed in India

Releasing the Play's Voice: Rod Wooden's *Moby Dick* at the RSC

Cicely Berry and Andrew Wade

1.

In his working of the story of *Moby Dick,* Rod has kept wonderfully the rolling, heightened prose of the original text: he has kept its salt flavour, the physicality of the language which takes us into a world beyond, a world of the imagination.

Because the language originated in a novel, ie it was created for the reader, it does not have the obvious energy/rhythm of dialogue – it has a different energy, and this presented the actors with a challenge – a challenge to find a way to preserve its rolling, cumulative form, yet make the text sound active in a spoken sense. And working as we did on this first production we found ourselves in uncharted water as it were.

Ahab is a character on his own who motivates the action, and so in a way dictates his own rhythm: and David Calder, with his innate poetic sense, responded immediately to the heightened and rhythmic language.

But the other characters and crew are very much part of a team: they have to create that communal world – the sea, the ship, the very rough male relationships – whilst keeping their own character identity intact: and this is particularly apparent in the writing of the Chorus. Here each actor has to find the rhythm of the whole expressed through his own character – for that world is contained in the rhythm as much as anything else: a rhythm which is not naturalistic, nor does it have the strict code of verse – but it is a rhythm you have to feel throughout your body.

2.

Let us take for example the wonderful Chorus near the beginning: the first part begins –

    'There is a galloping in the sea
    a galloping without hooves ...'
    like a tidal race
    or a sea-god's heartbeat
    can you hear it, Moby Dick ...'

We hear the galloping in the rhythm, but that rhythm very quickly changes to something much heavier:

    'Through rain-pelt and wind-lash
    through hail-clunk and storm-thrust
    I am coming ...'

And again this changes into these very simple lines:
> 'I hate white as a colour
> it's a nothing, a zero ...'

Now this Chorus is written in seven parts, and each part has a different rhythm, a different perspective, a different texture. We hear that texture through the different alignment and weight of vowels and consonants, for instance the sounds in the lines:
> 'Though rain-pelt and wind-lash
> through hail-clunk and storm-thrust
> I am coming ...'

have a totally different weight/texture to those in:
> 'I hate white as a colour
> it's like someone who vanished
> or a house that's left empty
> or a glass with no drink ...'

And the actor has to be sensitive to this changing movement within the language and honour it – he has to make us hear this world – yet inhabit it on his own terms.

3.

So, working closely with Gerry Mulgrew, the Director, our task was to help the actors find this rhythm, this imagery, while keeping their own very personal imagination intact and alive: it was essential that they felt truthful within it. And we had a very enthusiastic group of actors to work with – and very physical.

We worked roughly in two ways: one way was by speaking the Chorus round in a circle a number of times, taking a line each – slowly at first until we were familiar with it. This may seem simple, but it is not: for you need to do it many times before you can hear the precise rhythm of each line and hand it on to the next person, honouring its cadence and lifting it through. It is a wonderful exercise in listening – what you hear and how you hear it, and although it takes time, it is in the end very exciting.

We then set physical challenges: we gave each actor specific tasks to perform while speaking the lines. This is always a very freeing thing to do, because it takes the over-concentration off the words – ie the tension which comes from wanting to get it 'right ' – and also, because the actor is moving physically, the words are released often in a surprising way and we hear new rhythms, new meanings.

We alternated these two methods and layered them through the rehearsal period until the actors felt at home with both the muscularity and the musicality of the language: we then practised it *in situ* – ie as they had to move on stage – and this movement was physically exacting. I think the process was never easy: to be disciplined within the needs of the production, yet keeping the discovery of the thought alive and their responses to each other fresh in every moment, but it was a great challenge, and one that brought a great sense of unity within the cast – and also exhilaration. It was an exciting text to work on.

4.

Hopefully, this practical input enabled the beautiful, contemporary quality of the writing to be realised, and certainly it revealed to us the enormity of the challenge for a contemporary writer wanting to reinterpret the work, in modern times – unless one speaks the language of the elements. Rod achieves this and his success brings the subtle links between modern writing and classical theatre into light. Rod evidently writes with the awareness that – as in Shakespeare for example – meaning is never a given fact at the end of a statement. Meaning is born out of a totality of elements, out of the resonances of each individual word.In theatre, as we know, there is no turning back. Each word spoken by the actor is thrown into a sea of language. In Rod's writing, however, words often come back to us by the flux of the waves.

The play finds it relevance for the modern audience in its metaphysical implications, which also resemble Melville's. The world which we are given to hear in the play is one of anguished doubt. Melville's questionings have reached the core of our modernity: what if there was nothing behind the mask, behind the absolute whiteness of the whale? With the fall of most of our metaphysical certainties we too have become decentred creatures lost in our quest for meaning. When all else fails what are we left with but this our language?

Contemporary Theatre Review,
1996, Vol. 5, 3–4 pp. 159–163
Reprints available directly from the publisher
Photocopying permitted by license only

From Manchester to Chicago: The Journey of Rod Wooden's *Your Home in the West* from the Royal Exchange Theatre, U.K. to Steppenwolf Theatre, U.S.A.

Charlotte J. Headrick, Ph.D.

Oregon State University, Corvallis, Oregon

During my sabbatical year in 1991, I visited theatres in England, Wales, Scotland, and Ireland to interview directors, an occasional theatre manager, to talk to actors, to observe rehearsals, and, in the process, I saw dozens of plays. Thanks to John Doyle, then artistic director of the Everyman Theatre, my base was Liverpool. One day in early spring, Doyle returned from seeing a play at the Manchester Royal Exchange Theatre. He could not praise it enough. He said, "Now I know what it must have felt like to have been sitting in an audience watching the first production of John Osborne's *Look Back in Anger*."[1] He continued talking about how he knew he had witnessed a important event, the birth of a strong new play by a very important new writer. The play was *Your Home in the West*. The playwright was Rod Wooden who had already won the Mobil Playwriting Competition for writing the play. He was also awarded the 1990 Mobil Bursary to work as writer in residence at the Royal Exchange. A native of Norfolk, Wooden lives in Newcastle-upon-Tyne.

As an American academic, I knew I had to return to the Royal Exchange where, after touring the facilities, I had previously seen an adaptation of *Pride and Prejudice*. The matinee performance of the Austen piece was full of well-heeled, older individuals, what we Americans term "senior citizens." *Pride and Prejudice* was very pretty, solidly directed, competently acted, easy to watch, and just as easily forgotten.

John Doyle's assistant Daphne Bates and I travelled to the Royal Exchange to see one of the last matinee performances of *Your Home in the West* on April 10, 1991. What a contrast to the earlier production of *Pride and Prejudice*. It was not a full audience. In fact, the house was rather sparse. Prunella Scales and Timothy West were in the audience. Having been on the panel of judges for the Mobil Award, Ms. Scales told us that she very much wanted to see the play and because she and her husband were on tour with *Long Day's Journey into Night*, they had been able to sneak over for the matinee. Like *Pride and Prejudice, Your Home in the West* was also well directed and even more brilliantly acted. Unlike *Pride and Prejudice*, Wooden's play was neither pretty nor forgettable. It was riveting; there was not one weak

---

[1] Conversation with John Doyle, Spring 1991, Liverpool, England.

performance and the acting was marked by strong ensemble playing. That after-noon in Manchester was unlike any I had ever experienced. Everything "clicked." What also amazed me was that a male playwright was able to write such strong and compelling female characters.

The pivotal characters in the play, Micky and Jean, a divorced couple, are locked in a battle of wills, psychological warfare, gut-slicing and bloodless. The field of battle is a decaying run-down council flat in economically depressed New-castle-upon-Tyne. The chief trophies of war are Micky and Jean's two children. No knives are drawn, but words and memory are the weapons of choice. In the Man-chester production Lorraine Ashbourne and David Threlfall were fascinating to watch. My journal entry for the production reflects my strong reaction to the play:

> Magnificent script, riveting performances. It was such a good production. How do I describe this? A dysfunctional family living on the estates in Newcastle, in the depressed industrial north. This play is about anger, about frustration, about not being able to break out of a self–perpetuating way of life. I was shaking inside when the play finished. I knew I had experienced something important. I looked around me in the half–empty theatre wanting to scream... here was a script worth 10 productions of *Pride and Prejudice*. I want to shout to the rafters – I want to write the Oregon Shakespeare Festival[2]; I want to write Steppenwolf in Chicago that they must do this script. The performances <u>were</u> riveting.[3]

If the main criterion of great drama is that it lingers in the hearts and souls and minds of its audiences, then *Your Home in the West* is great drama. As the journal entry reveals, I left the theatre stunned. In the past ten years, there have been a dozen plays that have stayed with me, continuing to resonate, plays whose images, language, and actions trigger powerful reactions and emotions. The Royal Exchange production was a winning combination of strong direction, strong acting, but most importantly a powerfully written script.

Wooden's script received strong response from the critics. "It is a savage, sordid ghetto where children kill cats and life is as bleak as an east wind blowing from the Tyne."[4] The *Liverpool Daily Post* terms the play "powerful and earthy, it is some-times wry, it is always compulsive. At times the tension holds the entire theatre in a vicelike grip."[5] Bob Keogh calls the play "the most startling, even shattering, new play I have seen in a long time."[6] While noting it was a relief to escape into the night after viewing Wooden's world, critic Michael Schmidt notes "and yet to have seen that world so clearly portrayed is a rare and compelling experience."[7] The London *Sunday Times* calls Wooden a "Zola of the English north, but a Zola with humour and a black passion which should take him far if he keeps control of it."[8] Robin Thornber of *The Guardian* liked the play more than the direction and the

---

[2]   The Oregon Shakespeare Company is one of the most prestigious repertory theatres in the United States; in their three theatres, they have a commitment to new plays as well as their continuing dedica-tion to producing Shakespeare.
[3]   Unpublished journal, 1991, of Charlotte J. Headrick. Play entry number 26.
[4]   Patrick O'Neill, The dark side of a home in the west," *Daily Express*, 5 April 1991.
[5]   Malcolm Handley, "A Social Worker's Paradise," *Liverpool Daily Post*, 29 March 1991.
[6]   Bob Keogh, "Royal Exchange Theatre, Manchester: Your Home in the West," *Yorkshire Post*, 30 March 1991.
[7]   Michael Schmidt, "Newcastle Brown and acrimony," *The Daily Telegraph*, 29 March 1991.
[8]   *Sunday Times*, London, 31 March 1991.

performances: "Rod Wooden's prize–winning play is a fine piece of writing ....
Deeply felt and deeply thought,it's a powerful piece of theatre."[9] Jeremy Kingston
of *The Times* says the play is "tightly constructed" and is an "incisive drama."[10] *The
Independent*'s Jeffrey Wainwright mentions the script's "great physical force."[11]

In late April, about three weeks after I saw *Your Home in the West*, I left Liverpool
and England. On returning to the United States, I found that the images in the play
were very much still with me. I didn't even have a copy of the script. My first
impulse recorded in my journal was one that I decided needed action. My fear was
that the play would not be transferred to London and if it did not receive a London
production, the script might never receive the wide viewing it deserved. It was too
important a play to be lost.

Because of my faith in the play, in May of 1991, I wrote a blind letter to
the dramaturg of Steppenwolf Theatre in Chicago.[12] Having long admired Steppenwolf's work, and knowing of their commitment to new scripts and their fearless reputation, I mailed the letter. In it, I mentioned the plays I had seen over
the years at Steppenwolf and how I felt that *Your Home in the West* was a
"Steppenwolf" script.

For years I was associated with the Kennedy Center/American College Theatre
Festival, an organization that has a prime commitment to developing new scripts,
to nurturing young American playwrights. It is very difficult for a playwright to
obtain one production, much less two. Never before in my academic career had
I written a letter quite like that one. I wrote the letter and hoped for the best;
Steppenwolf would either act on my advice and contact the Royal Exchange or
dismiss me as an eccentric academic.

In the summer, I received a letter from Eric Simonson of Steppenwolf thanking
me for my letter and telling me that if I had not written them, they might never
have known of the script. He assured me that my instincts were right, that it was
indeed a "Steppenwolf" play and that the ensemble had agreed that they must do
the script. *Your Home in the West* was to receive its American premiere, inaugurat-
ing the 1991–92 season of the company.

In early November I received a letter dated 25 October 1991 from Rod Wooden:

> I would like to thank you for recommending my play to Steppenwolf
> Theatre Company – they rang me in June to say that they wanted to do it and on 26th August I
> arrived in Chicago to start rehearsals. The play has provoked a very mixed response from the
> critics (very positive from the *Chicago Tribune*, completely negative from the *Sun Times*) but
> audiences seem to have taken to it ...[13]

In late November, on my way to Atlanta, Georgia for an academic conference, I
arranged to stop in Chicago for three days so that I might see the Steppenwolf

---

9   Robin Thornber, "Your Home in the West," *The Guardian*, 1 April 1991.
10   Jeremy Kingston, "Your Home in the West, Royal Exchange, Manchester," *The Times*, 1 April 1991.
11   Jeffrey Wainwright,"Poverty Trap", *The Independent*, 2 April 1991.
12   Steppenwolf Theatre will begin its twentieth season in Chicago in the fall of 1995. It has made and
continues to make a major impact on the face of American theatre. It is one of America's finest theatre
companies.
13   Letter from Rod Wooden to Charlotte J. Headrick, 25th October 1991.

production. Eric Simonson gave me a great tour of the new facility and told me that no one had ever written a letter, recommending a play.

At the time in May when I wrote the letter, it seemed the only logical course of action; at that time, I did not feel that my university actors would be up to the rigors of the script. Later I did write Cynthia White, the dramaturg at the Oregon Shakespeare Festival (this time including a script), but to date, they have not produced the play.[14]

Steppenwolf had assembled some of its best for the production: Rondi Reed, Ted Levine, Estelle Parsons, and Tim Hopper.[15] In some ways, the production was similar to the Royal Exchange original; in other ways, it was quite different. Perhaps the biggest difference was the space. Steppenwolf was housed in its new space which is more or less a proscenium theatre, very much a contrast to Royal Exchange arena stage. Steppenwolf was built with major input from the acting ensemble so the space is very much an actor/director space, designed to be in close proximity to the audience, enabling the actors to establish intimacy with them. Such was certainly the case with *Your Home in the West*. The ever excellent Rondi Reed as Jean was as much an anchor for the production as was Lorraine Ashbourne in Manchester. Estelle Parsons was wonderfully crotchety as Jeannie, Micky's mother, as had been Dilys Hamlett at the Royal Exchange. Andrew Leman and Derek Walmsley were equally strong as the mentally deficient Maurice. Both Tim Hopper and Andy Serkis added warmth and humor to the play as the Irish charmer Sean. The most striking difference in characterization was between Ted Levine's Micky and that of David Threlfall. In Manchester Threlfall's Micky was full of disturbing quiet menace, his black-gloved hand clenching and unclenching, the muscles of his jaw doing the same action. Ted Levine's Micky was explosive, loud, leather-jacketed to Threlfall's expensive suit. With prowling sexuality, complete with grabbing his own crotch, Ted Levine made his menace open and clearly obvious. Threlfall's menace was more terrifying because it had such control. Tom Irwin's direction at Steppenwolf was sensitive and sure. In Manchester, director Braham Murray used a real child in the role of Michael. In Chicago, a large bundle doubled for the sleeping child.

In November of 1992, almost a year after the Steppenwolf production, Live Theatre in Newcastle-on-Tyne opened their 20th anniversary season with *Your Home in the West*. Wooden wrote me that it was good finally to hear the play with its authentic sound and actors able to do the Geordie dialect.[16] Max Roberts' Newcastle production received strong reviews. Brian Severs in *The Stage* writes, "A spade was called a spade and dramatic use of uncompromising language made for an electrifying evening."[17] The local paper *The Newcastle Journal*, says of the production:

---

[14] Whilst Cynthia has since left the company, she did comment on the strong women's roles in the play.
[15] Tim Hopper and I both attended the University of Tennessee in Knoxville, Tennessee. We knew many people in common but had never met before that night in Chicago.
[16] Albert Finney during a visit to Steppenwolf commented on the bravery of the company in tackling such a difficult dialect. Eric Simonson related that Finney said it was a difficult accent even for British actors to attempt.
[17] Brian Severs, "Your Home in the West," 26 November 1992.

The language is bracing, no punches are pulled. It won't be everyone's cup of tea and it's far from relaxing. But it's well-written, well-acted and damn good theatre. You won't see anything quite like it again.[18]

Peter Mortimer of *The Guardian* captures the feeling I had as I left the Royal Exchange Theatre in 1991: "his words send us staggering weak-kneed into the interval bar."[19] Later he says, "Wooden's remarkable writing may eventually need to gouge out more hope. But watch out for him."[20] Wooden's play deserves a London production; the Royal Exchange in Manchester, Steppenwolf in Chicago, and the Live Theatre in Newcastle are admirable venues, but the play's message needs to be heard in London.

Between the Steppenwolf production and the Newcastle production, Rod Wooden picked up another honor. He received the 1992 John Whiting Award for *Your Home in the West.* There is an old actor's joke: there are only one hundred people in the theatre and they simply move around a lot. One of the judges for the John Whiting Award was John Doyle.[21]

---

[18] David Whetstone, "Spectacular firecracker, bracing and quite unique," *Newcastle Journal,* 17 October 1992.

[19] Peter Mortimer, "Your Home in the West," *The Guardian,* 26 October 1992.

[20] *Ibid.*

[21] John Doyle left the Liverpool Everyman in 1992 and is now the artistic director of the Theatre Royal, York. He directed the 1995 Regent's Park production of *A Midsummer Night's Dream.*

Contemporary Theatre Review,
1996, Vol. 5, 3–4 pp. 165–167
Reprints available directly from the publisher
Photocopying permitted by license only

Playing in *Your Home in the West*

Estelle Parsons

I was invited to play in Rod Wooden's *Your Home in the West* in its American premier at the Steppenwolf Theatre in Chicago, Illinois. I played Jeannie, Micky's mother. The part was described to me as a one scene part that requires a leading actress. (We've all heard that before.) It is an accurate description. The audience ought to establish a relationship with Jeannie immediately for the play to work most successfully.

The play exposes, among other things, the very complex relationship of an adult son with his mother. The death of the Mother triggers the dramatic climax. Jeannie, unfortunately, dies after her first scene, but her body lies on the sofa through most of the third act.

I confess to giving the audience more than its fair share of giggles with the antics of a sick old lady who was actually going to be dead soon. But surely this is a quixotic thing to play – a person who is expected to die but not necessarily tonight. She might be having a last flush of energy and surely she is allowed a very vigorous sense of humour since she has precious little else left. It is possible to rationalize any behaviour and attitudes given the soon to be "given circumstances".

Since I performed in the play I have read Sherwin B Nuland's book *How We Die* and learned about playing dead. "When the human spirit departs, it takes with it the vital stuffing of life. Then, only the inanimate corpus remains, which is the least of all the things that make us human .... [T]he face begins to take on the unmistakable grey white pallor of death; in an uncanny way, the features very soon appear corpselike, even to those who have never before seen a dead body." The actress – I – had to be content and challenged by a first act scene as a sick old lady, death off-stage during the second act and a dead body on stage for the third act. This is all so typical of Rod Wooden. He takes a meat cleaver to what might be a conventional play and pulls back the skin. He insists on facing the deepest and ugliest realities in his work.

The play contains three elements with which the audience and actors must grapple. The Newcastle-on-Tyne locale and dialect, foreign to most; life in the projects, foreign to most paying audiences; and fully dimensional characters with whom the audience is invited to laugh and cry. *Your Home in the West* is described as tragicomedy. Very often in the theatre, the tragi-part or the comic is fulfilled, but not both. At the present historical moment the comic tends to be fulfilled and not the tragic; people coming together in groups laugh at the slightest provocation, often when it is inappropriate. Is this because daily life presents so many difficulties and horrors or because audiences don't know how to listen? I don't know. This is an observation made in Chicago and New York City.

Not all actors play tragi-comedy well. Tragi-comedy requires of actors courage to make people laugh without worrying whether or not they will cry in the third act. Many wonderful tragedians have not a shred of comic timing and many with comic flair have not the development to express tragedy. Without tragi-comedians, tragi-comedy doesn't look so good. In writing tragi-comedy, Rod Wooden hurls himself once again from the mainstream.

In the playing sometimes it is hard to know why people laugh.

Your Home in the West evokes a profoundly horrible "real life". Maybe the audience is initially gripped with confusion: what on earth is it and how should I respond? Confusion, ignorance and fear swirl around until repugnance or fascination occur. It is not easy to act.

It cannot be easy to direct. To put the play up in the usual short rehearsal period cannot be satisfactory because the characters are products of the most profound and deepest early life hurts. Playing the play would probably come most easily to a prison population where the level of hurt is deeper than one finds in people who have chosen acting for a profession. The characters in *Your Home in the West* did not have the luxury of choosing acting or anything else for a profession. That is the bond that holds them so closely together.

I had only one scene to act (alive) and a very clear structure for the character: penniless, lived off her body, gave up her sons, potty and vengeful, lived and living by her wits. She's old and sick and near death. I found a dilemma in the very early days of rehearsal. I was trying to carry the play forward with the dialogue but I realized that every word came out of these seventy two years of life – the tone, the colour of her words, would not ring true without unlocking a lot of her doors. Unlocking the doors of my own emotional landscape, usually so useful, didn't seem to be helping here. Jeannie put me in mind of Franz Xaver Kroetz' writing about the verbal expressions of his characters. They have been so betrayed in life that they have lost the ability to express themselves. My friend translates Kroetz: "Their problems reach so far back and have progressed so far, they are not in a position to express themselves verbally. Language doesn't function for them."[1] Here is a (delicious) special challenge which I enjoyed so much in acting Kroetz.

Jeannie's life force and her expression come in conflict and create a compelling energy. The best way an actor can get to this conflict is to have a very creative rehearsal period, trying anything and everything so that when performances begin a rehearsal history infuses not only Jeannie's line delivery but also the attitudes of the other characters toward Joanne. The best of all possible worlds would provide "as much time as it takes" (Joe Papp's way of doing things) for a director and actors to work together creatively. A condition of trust among the actors in the company would allow an ensemble to go the extra mile to deal with the extremes of potential and real behaviour which are the norms for the situations in the play. These extremes give the play first its comic and ultimately its tragic dimension.

We often hear that if a play requires greatly talented actors to be played effectively it is not a great play. *Your Home in the West* is the exception that proves the rule. Rod has pushed himself so far into the deepest dilemmas of human existence that it requires courageous and gifted tragi-comedians to fully realize his material. However, I saw a production of *Your Home in the West* performed by a group who

---

[1]   Kroetz, Note on *Heimarbeit (Cottage Industry): A Play in 20 Images* (1969). Translation by Erica Bilder.

had neither courage nor skills. It was most interesting to observe an audience deeply enthralled as the play unfolded and stretched on the sturdiest of legs.

My image of this character if mine, Jeannie, was a person of flab – from a lifetime spent without physical activity after her working days were over. It was 53 when I played her but I am of Swedish blood and healthy and fit. It was easy enough to create the flab with padding and wrinkled heavy stockings but I had such conflict between the spirit and the degeneration of this woman that my personal opinion is that it would be best to cast a person of 80 who could go for broke with the spirit only. Perhaps I will have the opportunity to give it another go when I am eighty.

It was extremely challenging work. I have a personal opinion that Rod Wooden walks on a suicidal edge of "unworkable" and "unplayable" which is what makes his work so exciting to watch, gives it such intense energy, and can make it so suicidally challenging to act. He is always willing to fail. I had to have the same willingness to fail. Maybe that is what tragi-comedy is all about.

Contemporary Theatre Review,
1996, Vol. 5, 3–4 pp. 169–172
Reprints available directly from the publisher
Photocopying permitted by license only

Rod Wooden : Plays and Dates

THEATRE

WAH WAH WAH WAH, WAH WAH WAH

Written:	October – December 1987	
Rehearsed reading:	January 1988	Paines Plough, Riverside Studios, London Directed by Madeline Bedford

YOUR HOME IN THE WEST

Written:	January – April 1988	
Rehearsed reading:	October 1988	Paines Plough, Gate Theatre, London Directed by Stephen Jeffreys
Completely rewritten:	September – October 1989	
Productions:	March – April 1991	Royal Exchange Theatre, Manchester Directed by Braham Murray
	September – November 1991	Steppenwolf Theatre, Chicago Directed by Tom Irwin
	October 1992	Live Theatre, Newcastle Upon Tyne Directed by Max Roberts
	October – November 1993	Live Theatre, Newcastle Upon Tyne (& national tour) Directed by Max Roberts
	February – March 1996	Cirkus Tigerbrand Stockholm Directed by Lena Brännström

MEDEA MEDIA

Written:	August 1988 – April 1989	

| Rehearsed reading: | May 1993 | Northern Stage, Newcastle Upon Tyne
Directed by Alan Lyddiard |

HIGH BRAVE BOY

Written: May – June 1989

Productions:	February 1990	Northern Stage, Newcastle Upon Tyne Directed by Andrew McKinnon
	January 1992	'Off the RSC' fringe festival, Stratford Upon Avon Directed by Linda Marlowe
	October 1992	'Off the RSC' fringe festival, New Grove Theatre, London Directed by Linda Marlowe

ONE HUNDRED FEET

Written: June 1989

| Rehearsed reading: | March 1993 | Durham Theatre Co, Darlington Arts Centre
Directed by Cliff Burnett |

WOYZECK (from the German of Georg Buchner)

Written: October – December 1989

| Production: | February 1990 | Northern Stage, Newcastle Upon Tyne
Directed by Andrew McKinnon |

DIAMOND

Written: April – July 1990

Unperformed

SMOKE

Written: June 1991 – April 1992

Scenes added: February – March 1993

| Productions: | November – December 1993 | Royal Exchange Theatre, Manchester
Directed by Braham Murray |

	June 1994	Amsterdam Toneelschool Directed by Meral Taygun

ANTI/GONE (a commission for the RSC Education Dept as part of the Antigones Project)

Written:	July – August 1992	
Productions:	November 1992	Darlington Drama Centre Directed by Jane Howell
	November 1992	The Other Place, Stratford Upon Avon Directed by Jane Howell

MOBY DICK (a commission for the RSC, from the novel by Herman Melville)

Written:	March – July 1993	
Productions:	October 1993 – January 1994	The Other Place, Stratford Upon Avon Directed by Gerry Mulgrew
	March 1994	Gulbenkian Studio, Newcastle Upon Tyne Directed by Gerry Mulgrew
	September – October 1994	The Pit, Barbican, London Directed by Gerry Mulgrew

SORRY ISLAND

Written:	January 1995	
Production:	March 1995	Durham Theatre Co., Darlington Arts Centre Directed by Cliff Burnett

EACH WAY AND MOVE (a commission for the Royal Court Theatre, London)

Written:	July 1994 – March 1995

Awaiting Production

SANCTUARY (a commission for The Royal Exchange Theatre, Manchester, from the novel by William Faulkner)

Written:	March – May 1996

Awaiting Production

PUBLICATIONS

Your Home in the West

	March 1991	Methuen Drama, London
Moby Dick	October 1993	Crimes Against Theatre, London
Smoke	November 1993	Crimes Against Theatre, London

TELEVISION DOCUMENTARY

Celebration: Your Home in the West
May 1991   Granada Television, Manchester

AWARDS

December 1990: First prizewinner, Mobil Playwriting Competition (for YHITW)

February 1991 – May 1992: Mobil Writer in Residence Bursary, Royal Exchange Theatre, Manchester

July 1992: John Whiting Award (Arts Council), for YHITW

Contemporary Theatre Review,
1996, Vol. 5, 3–4 pp. 173–174
Reprints available directly from the publisher
Photocopying permitted by license only

Notes on Contributors

Cicely Berry has been Voice Director for the Royal Shakespeare Company since she joined in 1969, working with actors on both Voice and Text. She also works extensively in other countries/cultures. Involved with the RSC's Education activities, she has worked extensively in schools, with both teachers and students to open out ways of working on a classical text, and in prisons. Cicely Berry has written three books the most recent of which, *The Actor and the Text*, is widely used in the theatre and deals with how modern acting approaches can relate to heightened language – both classical and modern.

Cicely Berry was awarded an OBE in 1985.

Maria Delgado is a lecturer in Drama Studies in the Department of English and History at the Manchester Metropolitan University. She is co-editor of the forthcoming *In Contact with the Gods? Directors Talk Theatre* (Manchester University Press, 1996), editor of *Valle-Inclán Plays: One* (Methuen, London, 1993), author of numerous articles on Hispanic and British theatre and Spanish film, and co-programmer of the Manchester Spanish Film Festival.

Charlotte Headrick is an Associate Professor of Theatre Arts at Oregon State University, Corvallis, Oregon, USA. She holds a Ph.D. in drama from the University of Georgia. Although she is primarily a director, she is also an actress and is a member of American Equity

Estelle Parsons has appeared in 41 stage plays, 14 television plays, 10 musicals, 10 films, 4 revues and 2 cabaret acts. She can be seen currently in ABC-TV's *Roseanne*, and on Broadway in Michael Cristofer's *The Shadow Box*. She has won an Academy Award (for her role in *Bonnie and Clyde*), a Theatre World Award, two Obie awards, the CUE Golden Apple, Drama Desk Award and received several Tony nominations. She was one of eight people who started the NBC-TV's Today Show. For two years she directed the New York Festival Players who performed free Shakespeare for New York City Public School students and their families, produced by Joseph Papp. She is a member of the Board of Directors of the Actors' Studio. Estelle Parsons was educated at Connecticut College and Boston University Law School and has taught at Yale, Columbia, Sarah Lawrence, Fordham and Vassar. She is the mother of twin daughters and one son and is married to a lawyer, Peter Lenard Zimroth.

Meral Taygun is an actress-director of Turkish origin, educated at Yale University Drama School ('69 MFA). She is a bilingual actress-director who was and still is performing in many countries of the world. Since 1986 she has been the Artistic Director of the Acting School of Amsterdam. Meral Taygun is a member of the Dutch Arts Council and the England-based initiative 'Artists Against Racism'.

Andrew Wade trained at the Rose Bruford College of Speech and Drama and has worked widely in different drama schools, including Rose Bruford College, and was Head of Voice at the East 15 Acting School, London, for five years. Andrew Wade joined the RSC in 1987 as Assistant Company Voice Director and in 1990 was appointed Head of Voice. He works with the company's three Stratford Theatres, two London theatres, the RSC Education Department, the Shakespeare Institute, and the Shakespeare Centre. Andrew Wade has been involved with the Theatre Centre Young People's Theatre since 1976 and is currently a member of the Board of Directors.

Rod Wooden is an award-winning English playwright. His plays include: *High Brave Boy*; *Your Home in the West* (Mobil Playwriting Competition winner 1990, John Whiting Award 1992); *ANTI/GONE*; *Smoke*, and a new version of *Moby Dick*. He has recently completed *Each Way and Move*, a commission for the Royal Court Theatre, London.

CONTEMPORARY THEATRE REVIEW
AN INTERNATIONAL JOURNAL

Notes for contributors

Submission of a paper will be taken to imply that it represents original work not previously published, that it is not being considered for publication elsewhere and that, if accepted for publication, it will not be published elsewhere in the same form, in any language, without the consent of editor and publisher. It is a condition of acceptance by the editor of a typescript for publication that the publisher automatically acquires the copyright of the typescript throughout the world. It will also be assumed that the author has obtained all necessary permissions to include in the paper items such as quotations, musical examples, figures, tables etc. Permissions should be paid for prior to submission.

Typescripts. Papers should be submitted in triplicate to the Editors, *Contemporary Theatre Review*, c/o Harwood Academic Publishers, at:

5th Floor, Reading Bridge House	PO Box 27542	3-14-9, Okubo
Reading Bridge Approach	Newark, NJ 07101-8742	Shinjuku-ku
Reading RG1 8PP or	USA or	Tokyo 169
UK		Japan

Papers should be typed or word processed with double spacing on one side of good quality ISO A4 (212 x 297 mm) paper with a 3 cm left-hand margin. Papers are accepted only in English.

Abstracts and Keywords. Each paper requires an abstract of 100-150 words summarizing the significant coverage and findings, presented on a separate sheet of paper. Abstracts should be followed by up to six key words or phrases which, between them, should indicate the subject matter of the paper. These will be used for indexing and data retrieval purposes.

Figures. All figures (photographs, schema, charts, diagrams and graphs) should be numbered with consecutive arabic numerals, have descriptive captions and be mentioned in the text. Figures should be kept separate from the text but an approximate position for each should be indicated in the margin of the typescript. It is the author's responsibility to obtain permission for any reproduction from other sources.

Preparation: Line drawings must be of a high enough standard for direct reproduction; photocopies are not acceptable. They should be prepared in black (india) ink on white art paper, card or tracing paper, with all the lettering and symbols included. Computer-generated graphics of a similar high quality are also acceptable, as are good sharp photoprints ("glossies"). Computer print-outs must be completely legible. Photographs intended for halftone reproduction must be good glossy original prints of maximum contrast. Redrawing or retouching of unusable figures will be charged to authors.

Size: Figures should be planned so that they reduce to 12 cm column width. The preferred width of line drawings is 24 cm, with capital lettering 4 mm high, for reduction by one-half. Photographs for halftone reproduction should be approximately twice the desired finished size.

Captions: A list of figure captions, with the relevant figure numbers, should be typed on a separate sheet of paper and included with the typescript.

Musical examples: Musical examples should be designated as "Figure 1" etc., and the recommendations above for preparation and sizing should be followed. Examples must be well prepared and of a high standard for reproduction, as they will not be redrawn or retouched by the printer.

In the case of large scores, musical examples will have to be reduced in size and so some clarity will be lost. This should be borne in mind especially with orchestral scores.

Notes are indicated by superior arabic numerals without parentheses. The text of the notes should be collected at the end of the paper.

References are indicated in the text by the name and date system either "Recent work (Smith & Jones, 1987, Robinson, 1985, 1987) . . ." or "Recently Smith & Jones (1987) . . ." If a publication has more than three authors, list all names on the first occurrence; on subsequent occurrences use the first author's name plus "*et al.*" Use an ampersand rather than "and" between the last two authors. If there is more than one publication by the same author(s) in the same year, distinguish by adding a, b, c etc. to both the text citation and the list of references (e.g. "Smith, 1986a") References should be collected and typed in alphabetical order after the Notes and Acknowledgements sections (if these exist). Examples:

Benedetti, J. (1988) *Stanislavski*, London: Methuen

Granville-Barker, H. (1934) Shakespeare's dramatic art. In *A Companion to Shakespeare Studies*, edited
    by H. Granville-Barker and G. B. Harrison, p. 84. Cambridge: Cambridge University Press

Johnston, D. (1970) Policy in theatre. *Hibernia*, **16**, 16

Proofs. Authors will receive page proofs (including figures) by air mail for correction and these must be returned as instructed within 48 hours of receipt. Please ensure that a full postal address is given on the first page of the typescript so that proofs are not delayed in the post. Authors' alterations, other than those of a typographical nature, in excess of 10% of the original composition cost, will be charged to authors.

Page Charges. There are no page charges to individuals or institutions.